国家林业和草原局职业教育"十四五"规划教材

酒店英语

曾 溅　吴静梅　张丹凤　主编

中国林业出版社
China Forestry Publishing House

图书在版编目(CIP)数据

酒店英语/曾溅,吴静梅,张丹凤主编. —北京:中国林业出版社,2024.8
国家林业和草原局职业教育"十四五"规划教材
ISBN 978-7-5219-2545-6

Ⅰ.①酒… Ⅱ.①曾… ②吴… ③张… Ⅲ.①饭店-英语 Ⅳ.①F719.2

中国国家版本馆 CIP 数据核字(2024)第 018675 号

策划、责任编辑:田 苗 赵㛹旎
责任校对:苏 梅
封面设计:周周设计局

出版发行:中国林业出版社
(100009,北京市西城区刘海胡同7号,电话83223120)
电子邮箱:cfphzbs@163.com
网址:www.cfph.net
印刷:北京中科印刷有限公司
版次:2024 年 8 月第 1 版
印次:2024 年 8 月第 1 次
开本:787mm×1092mm 1/16
印张:12
字数:272 千字
定价:52.00 元

《酒店英语》编写人员

主　　编　　曾　溅　吴静梅　张丹凤

编写人员　　曾　溅(广东生态工程职业学院)
　　　　　　吴静梅(广东省外语艺术职业学院)
　　　　　　张丹凤(广东轻工职业技术大学)
　　　　　　黄　放(广东生态工程职业学院)
　　　　　　许　燕(广东省外语艺术职业学院)
　　　　　　贺　丹(广州民航职业技术学院)
　　　　　　吴冬绮(广东环境保护工程职业学院)
　　　　　　黄宝灵(广东省外语艺术职业学院)
　　　　　　林　超(广东省外语艺术职业学院)
　　　　　　陈绮媚(广州市星河湾酒店有限公司)

PREFACE 前 言

近年来，国家大力发展职业教育，相继发布《国家职业教育改革实施方案》《中国教育现代化 2035》《职业教育提质培优行动计划（2020—2023 年）》等文件。《中华人民共和国国民经济和社会发展第十四个五年规划和 2035 年远景目标纲要》明确提出："增强职业技术教育适应性。突出职业技术（技工）教育类型特色，深入推进改革创新，优化结构与布局，大力培养技术技能人才。"随着全球化纵深发展和"一带一路"倡议的持续推进，国家对复合型技术技能人才的需求愈发迫切。职业教育肩负着培养多样化人才、传承技术技能、促进就业创业的重要职责，应当创新教育模式，坚持产教融合与知行合一，努力培养能够参与全球治理和适应新时代信息技术的具备专业知识、技术技能、语言能力的复合型人才。

本教材的编写目的是培养旅游管理、酒店管理专业学生及相关行业从业人员的英语交际能力和英语语言知识，可供高等职业院校相关专业学生作为专业英语教材使用，也可供相关行业从业人员培训使用。本教材在内容上涵盖了大型酒店经营管理中所涉及的前厅服务、客房服务、餐饮服务、礼宾、其他酒店服务、酒店英语面试等各项服务和工作情境，以及酒店从业者用英语进行交流的各项内容，特点如下：

1. 校企合作，深化双元育人理念

教材编写团队中既有一线专业教师，也有行业企业人员，使内容的编排更符合职场实际和企业用人要求。坚持以校企双元育人为基本思路，立德树人为根本任务，教材将课程思政的教育理念和岗位职业道德规范要求相结合，将国际酒店工作岗位标准与国家职业标准相结合，通过创设真实的工作任务培养学生工匠精神。

2. 工学结合，达成能力培养目标

教材从职场工作领域出发，根据酒店的工作流程、工作情景设计教学内容，共有 6 个模块，20 个工作情景。每个模块以酒店某一工作部门为载体，每个工作情景都从解决问题入手，完成最终任务为目标，侧重听说训练和工作技能培训，具有趣味性和可操作性。

3. 文化传播，培养学生文化自信

在教材内容设计上，设置 China Story（中国故事）栏目，每个模块围绕一个中华优秀传统文化主题，讲好一个中国故事。该部分内容编排语言简练，图文并茂，助力学生深入了解中国文化，并在工作岗位上传播中华文化，培养学生的文化自信，为作为对外经济文化交流形象窗口的酒店岗位输送既精通酒店管理专业知识又具备跨文化交际能力的高素质技术技能人才。

4. 角色代入，体验真实职场情境

教材的内容设计和安排体现体验式学习模式，有效激发学生的探究精神，提升学生主动参与的积极性。教材内容构成主要在模块设计上体现产出导向的理念。每个工作场景设计具体的工作任务，逐步引导学生获取和处理信息，让学生参与到工作任务中，为学生创造表达自我的机会，以激发学生学习主动性的"交际活动"为切入点，以情境、任务、合作学习为主要方法，学生通过工作场景和自身体验互动，将语言技能融入职场工作任务中，最终实现职业技能的螺旋式上升。

  本教材由曾溅、吴静梅、张丹凤主编，联合酒店行业专家陈绮媚和王乐、酒店英语课程学科带头人黄放以及高职院校英语骨干教师许燕、贺丹、吴冬绮、黄宝灵、林超共同策划开发并合作编写。

  教材在编写的过程中参考了大量的国内外教材、教学资源及企业资料，在此对原创作者及支持企业表示感谢。

  由于编者水平有所限，编写的过程中难免有错漏之处，还请各位专家、读者指正。

编　者
2024 年 4 月

CONTENTS 目 录

PREFACE 前言

Module 1   The Front Desk Service 前厅服务 1

    Scene 1   Room Reservations 2

    Scene 2   Check In 9

    Scene 3   Check Out 15

    Scene 4   Bell Service 21

Module 2   Housekeeping Department Service 客房服务 31

    Scene 1   Receiving Guests 32

    Scene 2   Housekeeping 38

    Scene 3   Special Service 44

    Scene 4   Laundry Service 51

Module 3   Food and Beverage Department Service 餐饮服务 ... 63

    Scene 1   Cooking Methods and Ingredients 64

    Scene 2   Service During the Meal(1) 71

    Scene 3   Service During the Meal(2) 77

    Scene 4   Beverage Service 84

Module 4   Concierge 礼宾 93

    Scene 1   Hotel VIP Service 94

    Scene 2   Convention and Exhibition 100

Scene 3　Providing Information ·· 108

Scene 4　Finance ··· 115

Module 5　Other Hotel Service 其他酒店服务 ····················· 125

Scene 1　Recreation Service ··· 126

Scene 2　Handling Complaints ·· 132

Scene 3　Sales and Marketing ··· 138

Scene 4　Guest Service ··· 144

Module 6　Interview 面试 ··· 155

Scene 1　Get to Know Hotel and Yourself ·· 156

Scene 2　Interview Criteria ··· 162

Scene 3　English Resume ··· 169

Scene 4　Orientation ··· 175

Module 1　The Front Desk Service
前厅服务

? Questions for thinking

1. What is the duty of the Front Desk?
2. Do you know the main functions of the front desk?

Goals

After studying this project, you should be able to:

√　Make room reservation for the guests.
√　Help the guests check in.
√　Help the guests check out.
√　Provide bell service to the guests.

Prepare for learning

Scan the QR code to learn the new words and take a test on.

扫码听音频

1

Scene 1　　　　　　Room Reservations

 Activity 1　　Activate Language Knowledge

A Look at the pictures related to room reservations, write down the correct vocabulary as quickly as possible

(1)_____　　(2)_____　　(3)_____　　(4)_____

(5)_____　　(6)_____　　(7)_____　　(8)_____

B Scan the QR code and listen to the conversation

扫码听音频

Receptionist: Hello. Garden Hotel. May I help you?

Guest: Yes, I'd like to reserve a room, please.

Receptionist: When would you like to stay here?

Guest: From the 14th to the 17th of this month.

Receptionist: What kind of room would you like, Madam?

Guest: A single room, please.

Receptionist: Wait a minute. Yes, we still have some single rooms available. There is a variety of rooms, from standard to deluxe. Which do you prefer?

Guest: Well, a standard room will do.

Receptionist: OK. Do you have any requests?

Guest: A room with overlooking the park, preferably.

Receptionist: Sorry, Madam. All the single rooms overlooking the park have been booked up. How about a room with a side view? It overlooks a quiet street.

Guest: That would be fine. What's the rate per night?

Receptionist: 400 RMB a night.

Guest: What services come with that?

Receptionist: Services include breakfast, a color TV, an IDD telephone and a computer with internet access.

Guest: OK, I will take it.

Receptionist: All right, a single room for three nights, from 14th to 17th. May I have your name and your phone number, please?

Guest: Cathy Cooper, C-A-T-H-Y, C-O-O-P-E-R. My phone number is 139****4321.

Receptionist: Thank you. It's all settled. See you on the 14th.

Task 1. Discussion with classmates

1. What types of room does a hotel usually have?
2. What services are usually covered by the room rate?
3. What will you do if the guests' preferable rooms have been booked up?

Task 2. Practice with teammates

What information should you get when reserving rooms for the guests? Tick the right options and list more.

(1) arriving date ☐   (2) room type ☐   (3) name ☐   (4) phone number ☐

___

C Read the passage on voice reservations

With the overwhelming flood of new technology, some hotels have stopped paying attention to the phone-call bookings. However, not tracking your voice reservations could be damaging your hotel's revenue and marketing strategies.

扫码听音频

Here are some reasons why you need to remember the importance of customer phone calls.

1. They help you gain a deeper understanding of your market.

You can use calls to learn about current and potential customers. You're able to hear the customer's concerns and questions in their own voice. This way, you'll be able to get a clearer picture of any issues your hotel is facing.

Note

track	v.	跟踪（进展情况）
revenue	n.	收入，效益
potential	adj.	潜在的
concern	n.	担心，忧虑

2. They may become more common than you think.

Travelers today have access to more information than ever. With this abandance of information comes increased potential for confusion or indecision when they need to contact a hotel or travel agent. If voice interaction is becoming a crucial aspect of your daily operations, it's essential to prioritize it just as you do other parts of your business.

indecision   n. 犹豫不决

3. They help secure cheaper bookings for your hotel.

The more voice reservations, the better. Because it means you aren't paying for the distribution costs to an online travel agent (OTA). Dealing with customers on the phone also helps to avoid booking cancellations because you can discern their problems and provide adequate solutions.

discern   v. 识别，了解

Decide whether the statements are true(T) or false(F) after reading.

(　　) 1. Some hotels don't think that phone call reservations are important.
(　　) 2. Phone call reservations enable hotels to understand the market deeply.
(　　) 3. Room reservations through phone calls will disappear one day.
(　　) 4. It costs less for hotels to have voice reservations.

D Language tip

英语中，对两种事物进行对比，可以使用以下句式：
1. 单音节形容词结尾加 er，表示更……。例如，deeper（更深的），clearer（更清楚的）。
2. 多音节形容词前加 more，表示更……。例如，more interesting（有趣的），more expensive（昂贵的）。
3. The more…the better, 表示越……越好。例如，The more voice reservations you receive, the better. (你收到的语言预定越多越好)。
4. As…as…,中间可接名词、形容词和副词，表示两者一样。例如，Devote as much time to it as you do to other aspects. 在这上面花的时间与其他方面一样多，as tall as…(与……一样高)。

Complete the sentences with the correct form of the given words.

1. The standard rooms are _____ (cheap) than the deluxe rooms.
2. The room rate of this hotel is _____ (reasonable) than that one.
3. The deluxe room is _____ (comfortable) than single room.
4. I will stay here as _____ (long) as I did last time.

5. The service in your hotel is not as _____ (good) as that one.

E Test yourself

Task 1. Put the sentences into the right order. The first one has been done for you.

(1) Garden Hotel. Can I help you?

(   ) OK. When would you like to stay?

(   ) If you wish I can put your reservation on waiting list or would you like me to recommend another hotel?

(   ) Yes, I would like to book a double room for two nights.

(   ) Oh, that's bad.

(   ) I am sorry. All our rooms are booked on May 20th.

(   ) OK. Please wait. I will check.

(   ) From May 20th to 22nd.

(   ) Please recommend another hotel to me. Thank you.

Task 2. Scan the QR code and interpret what you hear from Chinese into English or from English into Chinese.

扫码听音频

(1) _____

(2) _____

(3) _____

(4) _____

(5) _____

(6) _____

Activity 2 Acquire Serving Skills

A The serving skills—making reservation by phone

Step one: Answer the phone within 3 rings.

Step two: Greet the guests properly.

Step three: Ask about the names and when the guests want to check in and check out.

Step four: Highlight the different features of each type of rooms and their price.

Step five: Explain your procedure for guaranteed reservation.

Step six: Get contact details.

Step seven: Repeat all required information to be sure that you have made proper reservation.

Step eight: Thank the guests for their calling and finish the conversations.

B Dealing with reservation changes

When reservation changes happen, you need to communicate the following information with the guests.

1. The reservation number
2. The changed date for check-in and check-out
3. The changed room type
4. The changed room rate

C Special tip

Reservation confirmation is an acknowledgement given by the hotel to the guests for their room request and also the personal details given at the time of booking. A written confirmation states the intent of both parties and confirms important points of agreement like name, arrival departure date, number of guests staying, room rate, type of room booked, number of rooms, pick up details, details of the deposit made, package details etc.

Dear Mr. Smith

Thank you for choosing to stay with us at the Sample Hotel. We are pleased to confirm your reservation as follows:

Confirmation Number:	123456
Guest Name:	Mr. Ned Smith
Arrival Date:	10/15/22
Departure Date:	10/18/22
Number of Guests:	2
Accommodations:	Deluxe King Suite
Rate per Night:	3000.00 RMB
Check-in Time:	2pm
Check-out Time:	12am

Should you require an early check-in, please make your request as soon as possible. If you find it necessary to cancel this reservation, the Sample Hotel requires notification by 4pm. the day before your arrival to avoid a charge for one night's room rate.

We look forward to the pleasure of having you as our guest at the sample Hotel.

Sincerely

Wang Guiming
Reservations Department

Activity 3　Practical Training

A　Receive the tasks—role play

Task 1. Make room reservation

Helen Copper is calling Garden Hotel to book a room. The front desk agent is answering the call and making reservation for her. The information is as follow：

预定人姓名：Helen Copper
房间类型：单人豪华房一间
时间：8月12日到17日，共5晚
要求：房间安静，有国际长途电话、计算机和WiFi，24小时热水
有无其他设施与服务
价格与折扣
电话号码：139 **** 1245

酒店：Garden Hotel
房间类型：单人房、双人房、标准房、豪华间
设施：健身中心、西餐厅、网球场、游泳池
服务：叫醒电话、洗衣、订票、租车
价格：单人豪华间1000元一晚

Task 2. Change reservations

Sally is calling to make some changes to the existing reservation. The reservation agent is helping her to change the record. The information is as follow：

Reservation number：235645

Check-in date：change from September 15th to September 16th

Check-out date：change from September 23rd to September 24th

Room type：change from a courtyard room to one with a view

Room rate：change from 500 RMB to 600 RMB

Useful expressions

- I'd like to reserve a room for June 1st.
- What kind of room would you like?
- How long will you stay?
- What's the rate for a double room?
- Are there any special discounts for staying 5 nights?
- I am calling to make some changes to the existing reservation.

B Training card

Name:	Class:	Date:
Your role:	Partner's role:	
Your task:		
Your process:		

Conversation between the guest (your partner) and the front desk agent (you).

Activity 4   Evaluate Your Study

No.	Tasks	Self-assessment	Group assessment	Teacher evaluation
1	I can tell the procedure of making room reservation for the guests.			
2	I can ask and answer questions when making reservation and changing reservation.			
3	I can talk about the importance of voice reservation.			
4	I can talk about phone etiquette.			
5	I can master the vocabularies and expressions on room reservation.			

Module 1 The Front Desk Service 前厅服务

Scene 2 Check In

Activity 1 Activate Language knowledge

A Look at the pictures related to hotel check-in, write down the correct vocabulary as quickly as possible

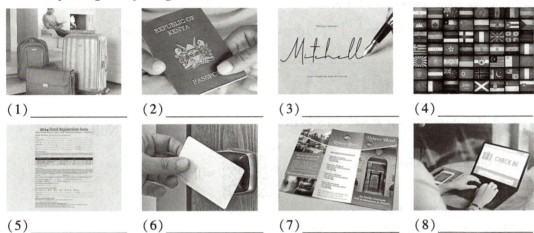

(1) _____ (2) _____ (3) _____ (4) _____

(5) _____ (6) _____ (7) _____ (8) _____

B Scan the QR code and listen to the conversation

扫码听音频

Receptionist: Good afternoon. Welcome to Garden Hotel. How can I help you?

Guest: Good afternoon. My name is Cathy Cooper. I have a reservation here.

Receptionist: Just a moment, please. I'll check. Yes, we do have a reservation deluxe room Cathy Cooper for 2 nights from the 14th to the 16th. One single room with a side view.

Guest: Can I check in now?

Receptionist: Yes, of course. Would you please fill in the registration form?

(*The guest fills in the form*)

Receptionist: Let me see…name, address, nationality, passport number, signature, and date of departure. Could you please provide your ID for verification?

Guest: Sure. Here you are.

Receptionist: Thank you. Now everything is in order. Your room number is 1232. Here is your key and a brochure with hotel service information. Please have a look at it.

Guest: Thank you.

Receptionist: Hope you will enjoy your stay here.

Task 1. Discussion with classmates

1. How do you receive the guests who have made reservations?
2. What do you need to check when receiving foreign guests?
3. What do you give to the guests after check-in?

Task 2. Practice with teammates

What information should you confirm when helping the guests who have reservations check in? Tick the right options and list more.

(1) name ☐   (2) room type ☐   (3) departure date ☐   (4) passport number ☐

_____

C Read the passage on hotel check-in

The hotel check in process has a pretty historical routine that is sticking around even to this day.

扫码听音频

Generally the process is:

1. The guests arrive and head to the front desk.
2. The guests is identified and have their details checked.
3. Front desk staff will give the guests an introduction to the hotel.
4. The guests will be handed their keys/keycard.
5. Luggages are taken to the rooms by the guests or the hotel staff.
6. The guests enter and settle into their rooms.

It's been roughly this way for so long that it's exactly what guests expect, but are they satisfied with a process that looks simple on paper but can become complicated and time-consuming? Nowadays, with new technology involved, travelers certainly love having options. When it comes to the check-in process, the guests will jump on anything that makes it easier on them. Remote or online check-in can save the guests a lot of time. Online check-in can be enabled through the hotel's website or via a mobile APP, making things simple for guests.

The majority of travelers are interested in checking-in

Note

historical	adj. 历史的
identify	v. 确认，证明
complicated	adj. 复杂的
time-consuming	adj. 耗时的
remote	adj. 远程的
majority	n. 大多数

online, since it appeals to their need for freedom and convenience. They won't have to worry about long lines or delays in service.

Decide whether the statements are true(T) or false(F) after reading.

(　　) 1. The guest need to be identified and has their details checked when checking in.
(　　) 2. The traditional check-in process has been applied till today.
(　　) 3. Check-in at the front desk costs less time than online check-in.
(　　) 4. The majority travelers prefer online check-in.

D Language tip

英语中，以下两种情况需要用被动语态：
1. 不知道动作的发出者，或没有必要说明动作的发出者。
   例句：The guests is identified and have their details checked.
2. 对动作的承受者进行强调。
   例句：Luggages are taken to the rooms by the guests or the hotel staff.

被动语态句式：主语+be+动词的过去分词，在具体的句子中，be 要随着数量和时态的变化而变化。

Complete the sentences with the correct form of the given words.

1. It's said that the long bridge _____ (build) in two months.
2. The stars can't _____ (see) in the daytime.
3. Which language _____ the most widely _____ (speak) in the world?
4. The lost boy _____ (not find) so far.
5. Last year a large number of trees _____ (cut) down.

E Test yourself

Task 1. Put the sentences into the right order. The first one has been done for you.

(1) Do you have your booking confirmation?
(　　) Sure, here's my credit card.
(　　) That's OK, I understand.
(　　) I do, here it is.
(　　) Are you here for business or pleasure?
(　　) We hold a 300 RMB deposit for security purposes. It will be refunded after your stay.
(　　) OK, thank you. May I have your credit card?
(　　) You should definitely go to the Guangzhou Tower while you're here.

(　　) I'm here for some business and some pleasure. I'll see some of the sights while I'm here.

(　　) Thanks for the recommendation. I'll visit the Guangzhou Tower for sure.

Task 2. Scan the QR code and interpret what you hear from Chinese into English or from English into Chinese.

扫码听音频

(1) _____
(2) _____
(3) _____
(4) _____
(5) _____
(6) _____

Activity 2　Acquire Serving Skills

A　The serving skills—check in process

Step one：Welcome the guests with a warm and sincere smile.

Step two：Request for the guest's names.

Step three：Check the availability if walk-in guests arrive.

Step four：Complete the registration form.

Step five：Collect the passports if the guests are foreign nationalities.

Step six：Take the signatures of the guests on the registration forms.

Step seven：Collect advance payment if necessary and issue a receipt to the guests.

Step eight：Assign the guests rooms and allocate a room key.

Step nine：Inform the guests about all the facilities and services which are available in the hotel.

Step ten：Note down if the guests requested for wake up call.

Step eleven：Update all the necessary details of the guests in the system.

B　Details of handling the passports

Collect the passports if the guests are foreign nationalities and need to fill the following details.

1. Passport Number　　　2. Nationality　　　3. Date of birth

4. Issue date of passport　　5. Expiry date of passport　　6. Passport place of issue

7. Visa Number　　　8. Issue date of visa　　　9. Expiry date of visa

10. Visa place of issue　　　11. Visa type　　　12. Purpose of stay

13. Arrived from which place and proceeding to which place

Scan or make a photocopies of passports, attach with the registration cards, and handover the passports to the guests. Submit a detailed report of foreign nationalities to the local police station.

C Special tip

Hotel registration forms are used by the hotels and resorts in order to keep all the information of their visitors. The visitors have to provide their detailed information such as name, phone number, residential address, the mode of payment and so on. These forms are filled out by the visitors in order to confirm their reservations of hotel rooms and other facilities of the hotel.

Registration Form			
Arrival Date	Departure Date	Room Type	Room No.
Surname	First name	Nationality	Occupation
Purpose of stay		Contact details	
Type of ID Certificate		ID Certificate No.	
Payment	☐ Cash ☐ Online pay	☐ Credit card	
I agreed to pay all charges incurred by me during my stay in the hotel. Signature:			

Activity 3   Practical Training

A Receive the tasks—role play

Task 1. Check-in with Advanced Reservation

Lily Collins has just arrived at Garden Hotel where she reserved a single room last Monday. She walks to the front desk.

Task 2. Check-in with Walk-in Guests

David Stewart walks in a hotel with his family. He wants two double rooms for three nights but he hasn't made any reservations. The front desk agent is checking the availability for him.

useful expressions

- Have you made a reservation?
- Sorry, sir/madam. There is no record on our list. Are you sure you've made a reservation?
- Let me check our room availability.
- Could you show me your passport?
- Will you fill in the registration form, please?
- Here is the key to Room 1232.

B Training card

Name:	Class:	Date:
Your role:		Partner's role:
Your task:		
Your process:		

Conversation between the guest (your partner) and the front desk agent (you).

Activity 4 Evaluate Your Study

No.	Tasks	Self-assessment	Group assessment	Teacher evaluation
1	I can tell the procedure of check-in.			
2	I can ask and answer questions when receiving guests with reservations.			
3	I can ask and answer questions when receiving walk-in guests.			
4	I can fill the registration form accurately.			
5	I can master the vocabularies and expressions on check-in.			

Module 1 The Front Desk Service 前厅服务

Scene 3 Check Out

Activity 1 Activate Language knowledge

A Look at the pictures related to hotel check-out, write down the correct vocabulary as quickly as possible

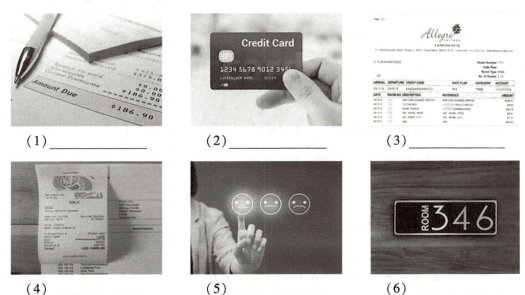

(1) _____   (2) _____   (3) _____

(4) _____   (5) _____   (6) _____

B Scan the QR code and listen to the conversation

扫码听音频

Receptionist: Good morning. Can I help you?
Guest: Yes, please. I would like to check out today.
Receptionist: OK, sir. May I ask your name and room number?
Guest: I am Tom Robert and I am from Room 890.
Receptionist: Wait a minute, sir. Yes, Mr. Robert, you are from Room 890 and you would like to check out today, right?
Guest: Yes.
Receptionist: Sir, have you used any of our service today?
Guest: No, I haven't.
Receptionist: OK, sir. Here is your bill. For 3 nights you have been charged for 1,500 RMB, 500 RMB for each night. The other cost is for laundry and room service you made during your stay. In total your bill is 2,000 RMB.

15

Guest: OK, can I pay by credit card?
Receptionist: Sure. By the way, how did you enjoy your stay in Garden Hotel?
Guest: Well, the room is clean and the bed is comfortable. I did enjoy my stay here.
Receptionist: Thank you very much for your comments. Have a safe trip home.

Task 1. Discussion with classmates

1. What is the check-out time for most of the hotels?
2. How do you help the guests to check out?
3. Is it important to collect the guests' feedback during the check-out?

Task 2. Practice with teammates

What information should you confirm when helping the guests check-out? Tick the right options and list more.

(1) name ☐   (2) room number ☐   (3) bill ☐   (4) payment ☐

_____

C Read the passage on hotel check-out

The check-out process is where the guests announce their departure from a guest room of a hotel. The word check-out normally refers to the departure or vacating of the room from the hotel.

The check-out process includes settling and clearing the bill of the guests and collecting guests' feedback. Some hotels provide express check-out facilities in order to avoid long queues at the reception desk. There are various necessary formalities during the check-out process to be done. The check-out peak hours start from 7 am to 12 pm.

At the time of guests' departure, the front office staff thanks the guest for giving an opportunity to serve and arrange for handling luggage. In addition, if the guests require airport or other drop service, the front office bell desk fulfills it.

Note

announce	v. 宣布，告知
departure	n. 离开
vacate	v. 空出，腾出
feedback	n. 反馈
express	adj. 快速的
formality	n. 正式手续
peak	adj. 高峰时期的
fulfill	n. 履行，实现

Decide whether the statements are true (T) or false (F) after reading.

(　　) 1. The check-out process is the guests arrive at a hotel and do registration.

(　　) 2. Collect the final payment and settle the bill for the guests when they check out.

(　　) 3. It is not necessary to collect guests' feedback at check-out time.

(　　) 4. The airport or other drop service is not included in the check-out service.

D Language tip

动名词由动词+ing 构成

1. 动名词作主语：

   例句：Swimming is a good sport in summer.（放在句首）

   例句：It's no use telling him not to worry.（it 为形式主语，动名词为后置主语）

2. 动名词作宾语：

   例句：The check-out process includes settling and clearing the bill of the guests.（作动词的宾语）

   The front office staff thanks the guests for giving an opportunity to serve.（作介词的宾语）

   We are busy preparing for guest receiving.（作形容词的宾语）

Complete the sentences with the correct form of the given words.

1. She didn't mind ＿＿＿＿＿（work）overtime.

2. She was praised for ＿＿＿＿＿（serve）the guests well.

3. He was thinking about ＿＿＿＿＿（make）a phone call to his boss.

4. ＿＿＿＿＿（collect）guest feedback is an responsibility for front desk clerk.

5. It's nice ＿＿＿＿＿（talk）with you.

E Test yourself

Task 1. Put the sentences into the right order. The first one has been done for you.

(1) Hi there. Are you checking out now?

(　　) The hotel isn't booked this week, so it's not a problem. How was everything?

(　　) That's no problem. It's always really busy at check out time anyway.

(　　) The room was great. The beds were really comfortable, and we weren't expecting our own fridge.

(　　) Yes, sorry. I know we're a few minutes late.

(　　) I'm glad you liked it.

(　　) Oh, really? The last hotel we stayed in charged us for a late check out.

(　　) No. I'll pay cash.

(　　) Will you be putting laundry charge on your credit card?

Task 2. Scan the QR code and interpret what you hear from Chinese into English or from English into Chinese.

扫码听音频

(1) _____
(2) _____
(3) _____
(4) _____
(5) _____
(6) _____

Activity 2　Acquire Serving Skills

A　The serving skills—check out process

Step one：Guest requests check-out.

Step two：Desk clerk inquires about quality of products and services.

Step three：Guest returns key to desk clerk.

Step four：Desk clerk retrieves hard copy of electronic folio.

Step five：Desk clerk reviews folio for completeness.

Step six：Guest reviews charges and payments.

Step seven：Guest determines method of payment and makes payment.

Step eight：Desk clerk inquires about additional reservations.

B　Details of arranging contact-less online check-out

1. Invite the guests to check-out online through their personal devices with a simple-to-use online check-out.
2. Inform the guests to check-out in the comfort of their rooms and pay any outstanding on-property charges on their bill by credit card.
3. Once the guests complete the online check-out, it will automatically update the OPERA PMS to change the status of their rooms.
4. Check the update status and make sure that the departure rooms are now empty.
5. Inform the chambermaid to clean the departure rooms.

C　Special tip

The **feedback forms** provide customers an opportunity to customers to provide the suggestions about hotel services. With the help of this form, the hotel management can get instant feedback from the customers about customer service. The feedback forms will provide both positive and criticizing remarks about the services of a hotel that will be very beneficial in improving the services.

Garden Hotel Feedback Form

We hope you will enjoy your stay with us! To help us better serve you, please complete this survey and return it to the reception desk at your convenience. Thank you!

Customer Name	
Address	
Email/Phone	

Statement	Agree	Neutral	Disagree	Strongly Disagree
My overall experience here was good, and I would recommend this hotel to my friends.				
The check-in process was timely and efficient.				
The check-in staff was courteous.				
My room was clean and comfortable.				
My room was furnished appropriately.				
My bed and bedding were comfortable.				
Housekeeping staff was friendly and reliable.				
Management was available to solve problems.				
The food quality was good.				
Room service was timely and efficient.				
Hotel amenities (pool, hot tub, exercise room) were clean, attractive, and properly equipped.				
The check-out process was timely and efficient.				
I received a complete and accurate bill.				

Activity 3　Practical Training

A　Receive the tasks—role play

Task 1. Check out

　　Mr. Brown is having his check-out at the front desk. He is complaining about the noise from the street.

Task 2. Late check out

　　The guest is about to check out, but he is a few minutes late.

Useful expressions

- Are you ready to check out?
- How was your stay?
- How would you like to pay?
- Sorry, we are a bit late checking out.
- We have a few complains.
- Enjoy the rest of your holiday.

B Training card

Name:	Class:	Date:
Your role:		Partner's role:

Your task:

Your process:

Conversation between the guest (your partner) and the front desk agent (you).

Activity 4 Evaluate Your Study

No.	Tasks	Self-assessment	Group assessment	Teacher evaluation
1	I can tell the procedure of check-out.			
2	I can ask and answer questions when helping the guests check out.			
3	I can deal with late check-out.			
4	I can prepare and collect feedback forms.			
5	I can master the vocabularies and expressions on check-out.			

Module 1 The Front Desk Service 前厅服务

Scene 4　Bell Service

Activity 1　Activate Language Knowledge

A Look at the pictures related to hotel bell service, write down the correct vocabulary as quickly as possible

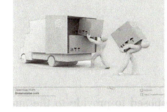

(1) _____　　(2) _____　　(3) _____

(4) _____　　(5) _____　　(6) _____

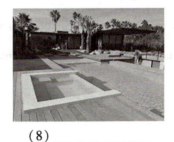

(7) _____　　(8) _____

B Scan the QR code and listen to the conversation

Bellman: Good afternoon. Welcome to Garden Hotel.
Guest: Good afternoon. I would like to check in.
Bellman: OK, this way to the Front Desk. Let me help you with your luggage.
Guest: Thank you.
(*after check-in*)

扫码听音频

Bellman: I will show you the way to your room. (Take the guest's luggage.)

(*on the way to the room*)

Bellman: This is the dining hall where you can have your breakfast tomorrow morning. The swimming pool is at the fourth floor.

Guest: I would like to know where I can do some shopping.

Bellman: There is a shopping mall on the left side of our hotel. It is about 300 meters away.

Guest: Thank you.

Bellman: Here is your room. If you have any problems, please call 001. Hope you enjoy your stay here.

Guest: Thanks again.

Task 1. Discussion with classmates

1. What is the main duty of a bellman?
2. What other services is a bellman supposed to provide to the guests?
3. Does a bellman need to have good product knowledge and good knowledge of the city and places of interest?

Task 2. Practice with teammates

What are the responsibilities of a bellman? Tick the right options and list more.

(1) transporting guest's luggage ☐

(2) storing luggage for the guests ☐

(3) delivery of food and other items to a guest's room ☐

(4) assisting guests with making arrangements for local activities ☐

C Read the passage on hotel bell service

Many tasks and responsibilities make up a bellman job description. Transporting guest's luggage is one of the main bellman duties. At luxury hotels, bell service staff are typically responsible for unloading luggage at curbside upon a guest's arrival, as well as delivering the luggage to a guest's room after check-in. Bell service staff also store luggage for guests as needed before or after check-in/check-out, and

Note

transport	*v.*	运送
luxury	*adj.*	豪华的
unload	*v.*	卸，取下
curbside	*n.*	路边
store	*v.*	保存，保管

usually load it directly into the taxicab or rental vehicle upon request.

Bell service at hotels also includes delivery of food and other items to a guest's room. Some hotels offer 24-hour room service, so guests can have a cheeseburger, a bottle of wine or a new razor blade delivered to their door even in the wee hours of the night.

razor blade	剃须刀片
wee hours	凌晨

Bellman responsibilities include assisting guests with making arrangements for local activities. They help guests buy tickets to shows or local attractions, make reservations at restaurants and arrange for a massage or spa treatment. Bellmen can also assist with getting a rental car, as well as calling for and to hail a cab for guests. Bell service staff often give advice on local things to do and see, recommending restaurants in various price ranges and local attractions.

attractions	n.	景点，名胜
hail	v.	呼喊，招呼

Decide whether the statements are true (T) or false (F) after reading.

(　　) 1. Greeting guests at the door is the main duty for a bellman.
(　　) 2. The only duty of a bellman is transporting guest's luggage.
(　　) 3. The bellman leaves guests the first impression on the hotel.
(　　) 4. The bellman should be very clear about the location of the facilities in and around the hotel.

D Language tip

help 和 assist 都表示帮助的意思，它们的用法是：

help sb do sth
They help guests buy tickets to shows or local attractions.

help sb with sth/doing sth
She helps me with my housework.
Bellmen can also help guests with getting a rental car.

assist sb to do sth
Good glasses will assist you to read.

assist sb in/with sth/doing sth
Bellmen may also assist guests with laundry service.
Bellman responsibilities include assisting guests with making arrangements for local activities.

Translate the following sentences from Chinese into English.
1. 我们将帮助他们克服困难。

2. 我可以帮您拿那些包吗？
_____

3. 她常常帮她的老板预定餐厅。
_____

4. 你将要协助大卫准备一份报告。
_____

E Test yourself

Task 1. Put the sentences into the right order. The first one has been done for you.

(1) I should tell you that I'm checking out in about 30 minutes.

(   ) You are so right, sir. The clock just struck nine.

(   ) Very good! Now, it's still morning here in Guangzhou.

(   ) A deposit? Isn't my luggage a deposit?

(   ) I'm sorry, sir, but it isn't. Your Master Card or VISA will take care of things nicely.

(   ) I'm ready when you are, sir.

(   ) Let me think about this.

(   ) I'm going to spend some time exploring the city. What can I do with my luggage?

(   ) OK, sir. But don't take too long. You only have 30 minutes.

(   ) Sir, right here we have a storage site. It's only 10 RMB an hour, but you need to leave a deposit.

Task 2. Scan the QR code and interpret what you hear from Chinese into English or from English into Chinese.

扫码听音频

(1) _____
(2) _____
(3) _____
(4) _____
(5) _____
(6) _____

Activity 2   Acquire Serving Skills

A The serving skills—bell service procedure

Step one: Greet all guests in the lobby in a warm and professional manner, make them feel welcome and anticipate their needs before they arise.

Step two: Recognize all returning and VIP guests, and welcome them back.

Step three: Escort all guests checking in to their accommodations following hotel procedure. Inform them about all hotel and guest room features, hotel facilities, and emergency procedures.

Step four: Assist guests with their luggage and acknowledge them by name.

Step five: Make deliveries to guest rooms as instructed.

Step six: Store and retrieve luggage and other objects for guests.

B Details of calling lift and showing the room to the guests

1. Assist the guests to call the lift by pressing the button to get the lift for the guests.
2. When the lift door opens, gesture with your open palm.
3. Explain how to use the room key to activate the elevator if appropriate.
4. Once the lift arrives at the floor, gesture the guests out first and then direct the guests towards their room as above.
5. Once you reach the room, open the door for the guests.
6. Demonstrate how to use the room key.
7. Open the door and gesture the guests to the room.
8. Ask the guests' permission to enter the room and ask if they wish to have an explanation of the room.

C Special tip

When storing the luggage for the guests, fill in a luggage claim tag and give it to the guests. The information on the tag should includes the guest's name, room, pieces of luggage, the date left and the date to pick-up.

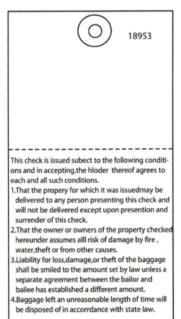

Activity 3 Practical Training

A Receive the tasks—role play

Task 1. Direct a guest to his room

A bellman is directing a guest to his room. He explains to him the facilities of the hotel on the way.

Task 2. Deliver food to a guest's room

A bellman is delivering some food to a guest's room as required.

Useful expressions

- Could I assist you with your luggage?
- Let me show you to your room.
- Let me tell you about our hotel facilities.
- Sorry to disturb you. This is the lunch you order.
- Enjoy your stay here.

B Training card

Name:	Class:	Date:
Your role:	Partner's role:	
Your task:		
Your process:		

Conversation between the guest (your partner) and the front desk agent (you).

Activity 4   Evaluate Your Study

No.	Tasks	Self-assessment	Group assessment	Teacher evaluation
1	I can say the duties of a bell attendant.			
2	I can ask and answer questions when greeting guests at the lobby.			
3	I can ask and answer questions when directing guests to their room.			
4	I know the etiquette for a bell attendant.			
5	Vocabularies and expressions on check-in.			

Chinese Story

Chinese Festivals

There are 8 traditional festivals very important in Chinese history, they are Spring Festival, Lantern Festival, Qingming Festival, Dragon Boat Festival, Double Seventh Festival, Mid-Autumn Festival, Chongyang Festival and Winter Solstice.

Characterized by diverse styles and themes, traditional Chinese Festivals is an important part of the country's history and culture, both ancient and modern. A close relationship exists between many of the traditional festivals and chronology, mathematics, the Chinese Calendar and the twenty-four Solar Terms. Many of the customs connected with the traditional festivals have linked with religious devotions, superstitions and myths. The form which most of the festivals take today was established around the time of the Han Dynasty (206-220BC) and for many years, various eminent poets have written countless masterpieces describing the festivals and are still recited regularly today.

Almost every festival has its own unique origins and customs which reflect the traditional practices and morality of the whole Chinese nation and its people. The grandest and most popular festivals are the Spring Festival, the Lantern Festival, the Qingming Festival, the Dragon Boat Festival, the Mid-Autumn Festival, etc.

A. Write down the names of Chinese traditional festivals.

(1)_____ (2)_____ (3)_____ (4)_____

(5)_____ (6)_____ (7)_____ (8)_____

B. Work in pairs. Discuss the origins and customs of each festival.

Festival	Origin	Custom
Spring Festival		
Lantern Festival		
Qingming Festival		

（continue）

Festival	Origin	Custom
Dragon Boat Festival		
Double Seventh Festival		
Mid-Autumn Festival		
Chong Yang Festival		
Winter Solstice		

C. Work in Team.

For celebrating the splendid Winter Olympic Game held in Beijing, you and your friends decide to design a poster to introduce one of Chinese traditional festivals for the athletes.

② Choose a representative from each group to present the poster and tell the reason you wanting to introduce this Chinese festival to the athletes.

Module 2

Housekeeping Department Service
客房服务

? Questions for thinking

1. What is the duty of the housekeeping department?
2. Do you know the main functions of the housekeeping department?

Goals

After studying this project, you should be able to:

√ Answer guests' questions.
√ Tell the main duties of a chambermaid.
√ Describe basic steps for room cleaning.
√ Know how to fill the laundry list.

Prepare for learning

Scan the following QR code to learn the new words and take a test.

扫码听音频

Scene 1   Receiving Guests

Activity 1   Activate Language Knowledge

A Look at the pictures of different items in guest room, write down the correct vocabulary as quickly as possible

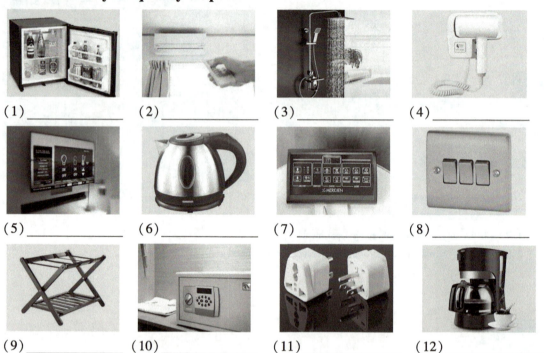

(1)_____ (2)_____ (3)_____ (4)_____

(5)_____ (6)_____ (7)_____ (8)_____

(9)_____ (10)_____ (11)_____ (12)_____

B Scan the QR code and listen to the conversation

Bellman: Sir, this way please. Your Room 1213 is at the end of the corridor, which is very quiet.

(*The bellman open the door, precedes the guest into the room and turns on the lights*)

Could I put your suitcase on the luggage rack next to the wardrobe?

Guest: Yes, please. The room looks so spacious and comfortable. Could you give me some information about your room facilities?

Bellman: Sure, sir. All our hotel rooms are equipped with mini-bar, IDD telephone, satellite TV, and internet connection.

Guest: Great. Is there hot water all day?

Bellman: Yes, there is 24-hour hot water for bath, but it is undrinkable. And there is an electric kettle for you to boil hot water on the table.

Guest: All right.

Bellman: You can find the mini-bar and safe in the closet. Some drinks and snacks are provided in the mini-bar. And there is a safe in the wardrobe, you can keep your valuables in it.

Guest: OK, I got it. By the way, do you know when room service is available?

Bellman: It's available 24 hours a day. There is a hotel manual on the desk, if you want to know more services in our hotel, you can find full information about the facilities and services in it.

Guest: Thank you very much.

Bellman: You are welcome.

Task 1. Discussion with classmates

1. How does the guest like the room?
2. Where can the guest get the information about the hotel services?
3. When is the room service available?

Task 2. Practice with teammates

Try to find out the correct information of room facilities which are mentioned in the dialogue.

Location	Room facilities	Functions
	luggage rack	
		boil hot water
in the closet		
on the desk		

C Read the passage on introducing hotel facilities

Nowadays, people choose to stay in the hotel not only for the accommodations, some of the tourists would choose a hotel because of its unique services or special facilities that other hotel might not provide. The more knowledge a hotel staff knows about the hotel facilities, the better service they will be able to give to the guests.

As a hotel attendant, you can introduce hotel services and facilities while accompanying the guests into the room. If the guests want to know how to use them, you ought to ex-

扫码听音频

Note

accommodation *n.* 住宿

facility *n.* 设施，设备

accompany *v.* 陪伴，陪同

plain clearly or show them. How to introduce a guest room and show the room facilities? Always be careful about the safety and security. While escorting, the attendant should point out fire emergency exit and fire extinguisher. Before entering room you should let your guests know how to use room key card. After the guests entering the room, you should open the window and switch on the lights and help him/her to put down the luggages. Then you can politely seek his/her permission to introduce the room facilities. Finally wish your guests to have a pleasant stay upon leaving the room.

security	*n.* 安全
escort	*v.* 护送，护卫
fire emergency exit	火警紧急出口
fire extinguisher	灭火器
switch on	打开
permission	*n.* 许可，准许

Decide whether the statements are true(T) or false(F) after reading.

(　　) 1. People choose to stay in the hotel only for the accommodations.

(　　) 2. It's necessary for a hotel staff to knows about the hotel facilities.

(　　) 3. While accompanying a guest into his/her room, a hotel attendant can introduce hotel amenities, services and facilities.

(　　) 4. If the hotel attendant want to introduce the room facilities, he or she should get the permission from the guest first.

D Language tip

当告诉他人不好或不利的消息时，可以用 **I'm afraid** 这一表达来缓和说话的语气，缓冲坏消息带来的冲击。

　　× I have to cancel the meeting.（语气太生硬）

　　√ I'm afraid I have to cancel the meeting.（语气更礼貌）

简短的表达：I'm afraid not / I'm afraid so

　　A：Can I pay by cheque?

　　B：I'm afraid not. Cash or credit card only.

Practice with your partner, paying attention to the manner of speaking.

1. **Guest**：My room is very small, can I upgrade it to a bigger one?
   Attendant：_____（no vacancies this evening.）

2. **Guest**：Are the snacks available free of charge in the minibar?
   Attendant：_____（be available at a reasonable price.）

3. **Guest**：Could you offer a better rate of my phone call?
   Attendant：_____（the best rate I can offer.）

Module 2 Housekeeping Department Service客房服务

E Test yourself

Task 1. Put the sentences into the right order. The first one has been done for you.

(1) Good morning, I'm Jason Smith in Room 1213. My shaver can not work, is it because of the different electric voltage? My shaver is operated by 110 volts.

(   ) I'm so sorry to hear that. We'll send someone to repair it immediately.

(   ) How much is the rental of a plug adapter?

(   ) Good morning Mr. Smith. I'm afraid so. Here is 220 volts in China. We will bring a plug adapter to you soon.

(   ) Thank you so much.

(   ) Great. By the way, the toilet doesn't flush.

(   ) It is free of charge.

(   ) You're welcome. We're always at your service. Please call whenever you need us.

扫码听音频

Task 2. Scan the QR code and interpret what you hear from Chinese into English or from English into Chinese.

(1) _____
(2) _____
(3) _____
(4) _____
(5) _____
(6) _____

Activity 2   Acquire Serving Skills

A The serving skills—introducing facilities & services

Step one: Escort guests and deliver guests' luggage to their room.

Step two: Keep in mind the price, all kinds of services, facilities and the newest room information of the hotel and always ready to introduce to the guest.

Step three: Answer guests' questions with enthusiasm.

Step four: Confirm guests' room and open the door for them.

Step five: Introduce the characteristics and functions of room facilities while getting the permission from guests.

Step six: Wish guests a pleasant stay before leaving.

35

B The common facilities problems in guest rooms

1. The air-conditioner is not cooling.
2. The electric curtains were breakdown.
3. The bathtub drain is clogged.
4. The electric scale has no power.
5. The water tap drips all night long.

C Special tip

When you start to prepare the guest room, make your guest room feel like home. There's something satisfying about helping your visitors feel welcome and comfortable. One way to understand your guests' experience is to assess your hotel based on the small touches that can make the difference. Ask the following questions during the review of your hotel:

Are the beds comfortable with soft and clean sheets?

Are there enough pillows?

Are the mattresses firm?

Is there a good supply of washcloths and hand towels?

Are the rooms kept at a comfortable temperature?

Is all the hotel information, such as the remote instructions and service guide, easily accessible?

Is there a clear space putting a luggage rack for setting down suitcases?

Activity 3　Practical Training

A Receive the tasks—role play

Task 1. How to use the safe

The guest does not know how to use the safe. The attendant gives out the clear instruction and show the guest step by step.

Task 2. Maintenance service

The guests call for maintenance service, because neither the air-conditioner nor the TV set works properly. The attendant asks for the details of the problems and makes a sincere apology to the guest, then promises send someone to repair the facilities immediately.

Module 2 Housekeeping Department Service 客房服务

Useful expressions

- Can you tell me how to use the safe?
- Set the code by inputting a six-digit password.
- I'm afraid neither the air conditioner nor the TV set works properly.
- We'll send someone to repair it immediately.
- Is there anything else I can do for you?
- We're always at your service.

B Training card

Name:	Class:	Date:
Your role:		Partner's role:
Your task:		
Your process:		

Conversation between the guest (your partner) and the room attendant (you).

Activity 4 Evaluate Your Study

No.	Tasks	Self-assessment	Group assessment	Teacher evaluation
1	I can guide guests to their room.			
2	I am familiar with functions of room facilities.			

No.	Tasks	Self-assessment	Group assessment	Teacher evaluation
3	I can introduce room facilities and hotel services to guests.			
4	I can handle the room facilities maintenance.			
5	I can master vocabularies and expressions on introducing room facilities and hotel services.			

(continue)

Scene 2　Housekeeping

Activity 1　Activate Language Knowledge

A Look at the pictures of different items in guest room, write down the correct vocabulary as quickly as possible

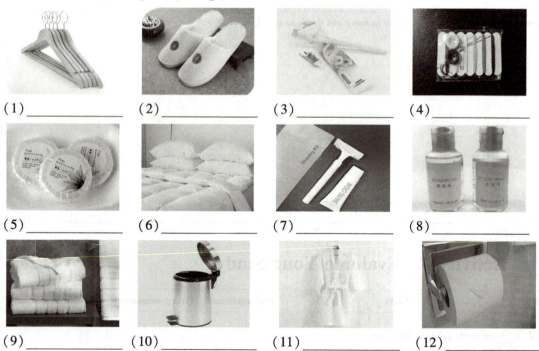

(1)＿＿＿＿＿　(2)＿＿＿＿＿　(3)＿＿＿＿＿　(4)＿＿＿＿＿

(5)＿＿＿＿＿　(6)＿＿＿＿＿　(7)＿＿＿＿＿　(8)＿＿＿＿＿

(9)＿＿＿＿＿　(10)＿＿＿＿＿　(11)＿＿＿＿＿　(12)＿＿＿＿＿

B Scan the QR code and listen to the conversation

Room attendant: Housekeeping, may I come in please?

扫码听音频

Guest: Come in.

Room attendant: I'd like to clean the room. May I do it now?

Guest: I will be out around 12 am. Could you come later?

Room attendant: I'm sorry, sir. No cleaning can be done between 12 am and 2 pm. When would you like me to do your room, sir?

Guest: It will be OK. Would you please come a bit earlier next time?

Room attendant: Sorry to keep you waiting. We usually have to clean the "check-out" room first, because we need to prepare the vacant room ready for another guest. Next time you may put the sign "Please make up" on if you want the room be cleaned as soon as possible.

Guest: I see. Thank you.

Room attendant: You are welcome. We're always at your service.

Task 1. Discussion with classmates

1. What kinds of room should the housemaid clean first?
2. What time can not do the room clean?
3. What should the guest do if he/she wants the room be cleaned as soon as possible?

Task 2. Practice with teammates

Write down the sequence of cleaning the following types of rooms during the peak season.

(1) Other guest room　　　　(2) check-out room

(3) VIP rooms　　　　　　　(4) rooms with "please make up" sign

_____　_____　_____　_____

C Read the passage on housekeeping

Hotels would find it impossible to run without a housekeeping staff. Most housekeepers work in specific areas of housekeeping, including the laundry room, ironing and laundering towels and sheets, and cleaning rooms or other hotel areas.

Housekeeping is responsible for maintaining high cleaning standards of the guest rooms and public area. The personnel here include housekeeper, chambermaid, room attendant, floor clerks and laundryman. Floor clerks, housemaids and room boys directly contact with the guests

扫码听音频

Note

staff	n. 职员
launder	v. 洗烫(衣服)
maintain	v. 保持；维持
contact with	接触

and contribute to the guests' overall experience with the hotel.

Room setting is essential when preparing a room for hotel guests. The hotel guests must feel comfortable on entering a clean and well-ordered room. Many hotels add special touches, such as luxury bath products, room design or bedding, that set them apart from other hotels. Housekeepers must arrange these special touches to specifications required by the hotel. Other duties may include folding and hanging towels in an appealing design, arranging a wet bar or turning down the bed and adding chocolate.

contribute to	有助于；促成
arrange	v. 安排

Decide whether the statements are true(T) or false(F) after reading.

(   ) 1. A hotel can be run without housekeeping staffs.

(   ) 2. Housekeeping staffs should not contact with guests directly.

(   ) 3. The environment that is clean and well-ordered will make guests feel very pleased with the hotel.

(   ) 4. Housekeeping staffs are only in charge of cleaning all the guest rooms.

D Language tip

1. 表示必须做某事时，用"must"或"have to"，例句：You must/have to clean the room every day.
2. 表示不必做某事时，用"don't have to"，例句：You don't have to change the sheets every day.
3. 用"must not"或"mustn't"来表示某人一定不能或不要做某事，例句：You mustn't/must not clean the TV screen with water.
4. 用"Do I have to…?"来提出疑问。

Choose the correct verbs to complete the sentences.

1. Make sure that you **clean / cleaning** under the bed.
2. Don't forget **dusting / to dust** the mirror in the bedroom.
3. You must **change / to change** the pillowcases every day.
4. You **don't have / don't have to** change the sheets every day.
5. Dust and **polish / polishing** all the surfaces.

Module 2　Housekeeping Department Service 客房服务

E Test yourself

Task 1. Put the sentences into the right order. The first one has been done for you.

(1) Room service. Can I help you?
(   ) I'd like a continental breakfast.
(   ) Good morning. Can I order some room service?
(   ) Coffee. Could I have a cappuccino?
(   ) It's Room 6503.
(   ) Of course. What would you like?
(   ) Very good. Would you like tea or coffee?
(   ) Certainly. Could I have your room number, please?
(   ) It'll be with you in ten minutes.
(   ) Thank you and goodbye.
(   ) Goodbye.

Task 2. Scan the QR code and interpret what you hear from Chinese into English or from English into Chinese.

(1) _____
(2) _____
(3) _____
(4) _____
(5) _____
(6) _____

Activity 2　Acquire Serving Skills

A The serving skills—room cleaning procedure

Step one：Knock at the door gently three times.

Step two：Say："Housekeeping."

Step three：Ask the guest whether you can come into the room.

Step four：Greet the guest.

Step five：Ask the guest whether you can clean the room now.

Step six：Begin the cleaning.

Step seven：Say goodbye to the guest.

Step eight：Fill in the room cleaning form.

B The details when do the cleaning

1. Make sure every room have toilet rolls at all time.
2. Don't have to change the sheets every day, but if a guest is staying for more than three nights, the sheets must be changed on the fourth day.
3. Remove used towels and replace them with fresh ones properly.
4. Ashtrays and wastebaskets must be properly emptied.
5. Floors and carpets should be thoroughly vacuumed.
6. Be sure the guest does not run out of soap or toilet tissue.

C Special tip

When there is a DND(Do Not Disturb) sign on the door knob or the door is double locked inside, return later or leave a Notice for DND guests which informs the guests that they can call the Service Center when they want the room done.

Sample:

> **NOTICE**
>
> Room No: _____
> Dear Guests,
> We have been unable to make up your room by _____ (time) because:
>
> • The do-not-disturb sign was on the door. ☐
>
> • The door was double-locked from the inside. ☐
>
> Please call our Service Center on ext. "9" to let us know at which time you would like the service or if you will not require service today.
> Thank you!

Activity 3 Practical Training

A Receive the tasks—role play

Task 1. Adding an extra bed

Mr. White's elder son who is 14 years old needs an extra bed. He calls the housekeeping department for adding an extra bed. According to hotel policy, the child under 12 is charged half the price, and a teenager is charged as an adult. The full rate of the extra bed is 34 US dollars.

Module 2 Housekeeping Department Service 客房服务

Task 2. Cleaning service

Housemaid greets the guest and ask the guest whether the room can be cleaned now. The guest doesn't want the room to be cleaned at the moment. The housemaid asks what time will be better to clean the room. The guest tell the housemaid to come at 11 am.

Useful expressions

- Could you offer me an extra bed?
- How much an extra bed costs?
- When would you like me to do your room, sir?
- If you need any help, just dial 3 or press the button over there.
- We will also provide another set of guest supplies in the room.
- I will let the overnight staff to make up your room.

B Training card

Name:	Class:	Date:
Your role:	Partner's role:	

Your task:

Your process:

Conversation between the guest (your partner) and the housemaid (you).

Activity 4 Evaluate Your Study

No.	Tasks	Self-assessment	Group assessment	Teacher evaluation
1	I can tell the main duties of a chambermaid on chamber service.			

No.	Tasks	Self-assessment	Group assessment	Teacher evaluation
2	I can tell the room cleaning procedure.			
3	I can leave a notice for DND guests.			
4	I can tell the details of making up the room.			
5	I can master vocabularies and expressions on chamber service.			

Scene 3   Special Service

Activity 1   Activate Language Knowledge

A Look at the pictures of different items in guest room, write down the correct vocabulary as quickly as possible

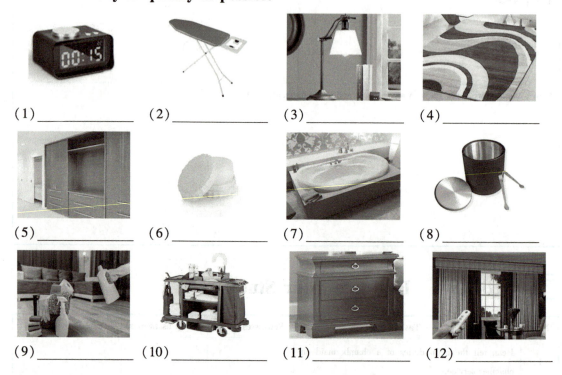

(1) _____   (2) _____   (3) _____   (4) _____

(5) _____   (6) _____   (7) _____   (8) _____

(9) _____   (10) _____   (11) _____   (12) _____

Module 2 Housekeeping Department Service 客房服务

B Scan the QR code and listen to the conversation.

Room attendant: Good evening, turn-down service. May I come in?
Guest: Come in, please. But I'm waiting for my friends. Could you come back later?
Room attendant: Certainly, sir. When would you like me to turn down your bed?
Guest: 9:30 pm. would be fine.
Room attendant: All right. I will come back at 9:30 am. Is there anything else I can do for you?
Guest: I want to know if you have the baby-sitting service.
Room attendant: We do have the service. You may call the housekeeping department to ask for special service. They will arrange it for you.
Guest: That's good. How about the charge for this service?
Room attendant: According to hours. The housekeeping department will give you the details.
Guest: Thank you.
Room attendant: You are welcome.

Task 1. Discussion with classmates

1. If a guest asks you to postpone the turn-down service, what will you respond?
2. What kind of special service the guest ask for?
3. How does hotel charge for special service?

Task 2. Practice with teammates

Discuss and list some special services that will impress guests.

Example: Services for wedding anniversary.

(1) _____   (2) _____
(3) _____   (4) _____
(5) _____   (6) _____

C Read the passage on providing special services

Today, some hotels try to provide guests a unique experience by some special services, such as turn-down service, wake-up call service, baby-sitting service, room service and transport service according to guests' different needs.

Turn-down service is the practical action of an attendant who enters a guest room to turn down the bed linen, clean

Note

| unique | adj. 独一无二的 |

and refresh the room. And wake-up call service keeps calling every five minutes until you actually confirm that you're up. More than that, to create memorable experience for guests, some hotels even personalize wake-up call service that not only wishes guests a great day, but also offers a cup of coffee to get guests day started. While a couple are celebrating their wedding anniversary at a hotel, they are surprised to receive a bottle of champagne or chocolate covered strawberries for them upon arrival. These small gestures will surely be remembered and appreciated by the guests.

  A good service is an act of respect, kindness and love which can be said to be the heart of the hospitality industry. Special services in hotels ensure that guests will come back for more and post positive reviews.

refresh	v. 使清新
confirm	v. 确认
personalize	v. 个性化
gesture	n. 举动，表示
appreciate	v. 感谢
review	n. 评论

Decide whether the statements are true(T) or false(F) after reading.

( ) 1. Some special services provided by hotel offer guests a unique experience.

( ) 2. Some hotels personalize the wake-up call service by offering a cup of coffee to get guests day started.

( ) 3. Special services will not surely be remembered and appreciated by the guests.

( ) 4. All services can be regarded as the respect, kindness and love to guests.

D Language tip

语言交流的过程中，需要委婉地表达否定、消极的情感时，考虑用"a little""a bit""a little bit""slight""slightly""small""one or two"等中性量化词来代替，降低对方对消极信息带来的焦虑。

  × There is a wait for a table right now.

  √ There is a little wait for a table right now. ("a little"会弱化否定的表达，使听者觉得更有礼貌)

Rewrite the following sentences.

1. We are having a problem with your credit card. (small)

_____

2. We're going to run over budget. (slightly)

_____

Module 2 Housekeeping Department Service 客房服务

3. There are many problems with your reservation information. (one or two)
_____

4. The launch plans are behind schedule. (a little bit)
_____

E Test yourself

Task 1. Put the sentences into the right order. The first one has been done for you.

(1) Good afternoon, housekeeping. What can I do for you?
(   ) This is a good idea. But my wife is coming here, I need to ask for a service to pick her up at tomorrow morning.
(   ) I'm John Smith from Room 1208. Do you have a service for wedding anniversary? I want to give my wife a surprise.
(   ) OK, Mr. Smith. May I have the information of the flight?
(   ) We will ensure you the time and will inform you the chauffeur's name in a few minute.
(   ) You are welcome.
(   ) Thank you for your consideration.
(   ) Mr. Smith, we do have the special service. We advice you reserve a romantic dinner preparing flowers, music and wine. And our hotel will provide some complimentary gifts for her as well.
(   ) Her flight AC877 from Seoul will arrive at 10 am in Baiyun airport.

Task 2. Scan the QR code and interpret what you hear from Chinese into English or from English into Chinese.

扫码听音频

(1) _____
(2) _____
(3) _____
(4) _____
(5) _____
(6) _____

Activity 2 Acquire Serving Skills

A The serving skills—turn-down service procedure

Step one: Knock at the door gently three times.

Step two: Say "Housekeeping, turn-down service".

Step three: Greet the guest if he / she is in the room.

Step four: Begin the turn-down service with the approval of the guest.

47

Step five: Clean the room and the bathroom.
Step six: Turn down the bed.
Step seven: Check around to make sure everything is done.
Step eight: Leave the room with expressing the wishes to the guest.

B The details when do the turn-down service

1. Check first if there is anyone in the room. Check the status of the room from assignment sheet.
2. If DND sign is hung on the door knob then take note of those DND rooms and return to them before going to off duty.
3. If the guest refuses then politely ask when you can return.
4. If the guest doesn't want turn-down service then politely ask does he need anything: "OK, sir. Would you like to have any fresh towel or any additional supplies like tea or coffee or bottle of water?"
5. Remove all trays, empty glasses or bottles, remove wet towels and empty the trash.
6. Place client things in order with discretion.
7. Create pleasing atmosphere by closing the curtains, turning off all the lights except for a bed side lamp, and spraying some air freshener as guests wish.
8. Before leaving the room recheck to make sure everything is in place.

C Special tip

Room service is a convenience. It allows guests to eat in privacy or outside of regular restaurant hours. Room service also saves time. Guests can get ready in the morning while their food is prepared. There are mainly two ways to book room service. One is to book by phone and the other is to use the doorknob menu. Doorknob menu is a type of room service menu that a housekeeper leave in the guest room, and often lists a limited number of breakfast items and times of the day that the meal can be served.

Sample:

Washington House Inn
Continental Breakfast
7 am to 10 am

Please join us in the gathering room for our expanded continental breakfast.

~ Or ~

If you prefer room service, please choose from the selections below.

Module 2 Housekeeping Department Service 客房服务

Place this card outside of your door by midnight.
—Granola (with milk)
—Seasonal fresh fruit
—homemade bakery
—Toasted bagel with cream cheese
—French-squeezed orange juice
—Coffee or tea_____

☐ Regular   ☐ Cream   ☐ Decaf   ☐ Sugar

Name_____
Number for breakfast _____
Room number _____

Your breakfast will be delivered within 15 minutes of the desired time.

Activity 3 Practical Training

A Receive the tasks—role play

Task 1. Turn-down service

The housemaid is going to turn down the bed for Mr. White now. Mr. White agrees her to do now. After finishing the turn-down service, Mr. White asks for two more cups.

Task 2. Room service

Mary Jones is staying at Garden Hotel. It is 4 o'clock in the afternoon. He is in the middle of a meeting with his two clients in Room 1003. They are hungry and would like to call the housekeeping department for a room service. They would like some grapefruit juice, marmalade, two scrambled eggs with two sausages, toast, and a pot of black coffee.

Useful expressions

- Good evening, turn-down service. May I come in?
- Sir, is there anything I can do for you?
- How much an extra bed costs?
- This is Room 1003. I'd like to have breakfast in my room, please.
- Sure, sir, what would you like to have?
- Your order will arrive in 15 minutes.

B Training card

Name:	Class:	Date:
Your role:	Partner's role:	
Your task:		
Your process:		

Conversation between the guest (your partner) and the housemaid (you).

Activity 4　　Evaluate Your Study

No.	Tasks	Self-assessment	Group assessment	Teacher evaluation
1	I can tell the main duties of turn-down service and wake-up call service.			
2	I can tell the details on turn-down service procedure.			
3	I can guide guests to the special service.			
4	I can tell the details of all kind of special service.			
5	I can master vocabularies and expressions on chamber special service.			

Module 2 Housekeeping Department Service 客房服务

Scene 4   Laundry Service

Activity 1   Activate Language Knowledge

A Look at the pictures of laundry symbols, match the correct expressions with the right pictures as quickly as possible

(　) dry-clean
(　) compatible with any dry cleaning methods
(　) dry
(　) do not wring
(　) hand-wash only
(　) no steam
(　) do not dry
(　) iron
(　) tumble dry with low heat
(　) normal wash
(　) wash with warm water
(　) do not iron
(　) wash with cold water
(　) delicate/gentle wash
(　) tumble dry with medium heat
(　) wash with hot water
(　) iron on medium heat
(　) permanent press
(　) tumble dry with high heat
(　) iron on low heat
(　) normal dry
(　) do not bleach
(　) do not dry-clean
(　) iron on high heat
(　) line dry
(　) any bleach when needed
(　) drip dry
(　) dry flat

B **Scan the QR code and listen to the conversation**

扫码听音频

Receptionist: Good morning, housekeeping. What can I do for you?
Guest: I'm Mary Smith in Room 1806. Do you have any laundry service?
Receptionist: Yes. If you have any laundry, please just put it in the laundry bag. The attendant will come and collect it.
Guest: Could you send someone to get it?
Receptionist: Sure, Miss Smith. I will send a valet to your room now.

(*After a while*)

Valet: Good morning, Miss Smith. May I have your laundry?
Guest: Yes, come in. Here is my dress.
Valet: Madam, please fill out the laundry list first.
Guest: All right. How do you charge for it?
Valet: There are details on the list. The charge is different according to the service itself.
Guest: OK, I see. When can I get it back?
Valet: It's 11 o'clock. If you choose express service, we will deliver it to your room at 3pm. this afternoon.
Guest: That's terrific. Is it more expensive?
Valet: Yes. We charge 50% more for express on normal service basis.
Guest: Well, may I have my dress dry cleaned and ironed? There is a few stains on it.
Valet: Sure, you can notify in the laundry list. How would you like to pay for it, madam?
Guest: I'd like to put it on the room rate.
Valet: OK. Please fill out the list and sign your name.
Guest: Here you are.
Valet: Thank you Miss Smith. Goodbye.

Task 1. Discussion with classmates

1. Where should the guest put the laundry if he/she need the laundry service?
2. What's the price of express service?
3. How do the guest pay for the laundry service in the dialogue?

Task 2. Practice with teammates

Listen to the above conversation again and try to find out what expressions are used to explain the laundry service.

1. By using a normal laundry price, in case of any compensation, we will strictly follow the rules stated in our _____.
2. Generally speaking, the laundry will be back the next day. If you choose _____ it takes only 3 hours.

3. Put your laundry in the _____ and fill out the laundry list. We will send someone to _____ it.

C Read the passage on laundry service

We know that most hotels, especially the exclusive and extravagant ones, offer laundry service. There are four types of laundry service which are the same day service, express service, next-day service and express pressing service. If the guest wants to get the dirty clothes laundered, he or she has to go through the laundry list, then he has to fill it up.

The process of laundry service is a multi-step one, including collecting, sorting, washing, drying, ironing, finishing/folding, and distributing. When collecting, housekeeping staff brings the dirty linens and clothes together to the laundry site. At sorting stage, the laundrymen sort the dirty linens and clothes in terms of item types. Moving to the washing step, the sorted linens and clothes is often required different washing formulas. And the laundryman should monitor washing times, washing temperatures, chemicals and etc. After washing, the clean linens and clothes are dried, ironed and folded. Finally, delivery people transport the clean linens and clothes back to the guests.

Staying in a hotel that offers laundry service is a big relief, because you don't need to pack too many clothes and you can have your clothes fresh and clean all the time.

Note

exclusive	*adj.* 高级的
extravagant	*adj.* 奢侈的
launder	*v.* 洗烫（衣物）
multi-step	*adj.* 多步骤的
sort	*v.* 排序、分类
distribute	*v.* 发放、分配
formula	*n.* 公式，程序
monitor	*v.* 监控，检查
delivery	*n.* 传送，交付
relief	*n.* 轻松，减缓

Task 1. Do it on your own.

Read the passage and try to figure out the process of laundry service in hotel.

sorting   distributing/delivering   collecting   washing
drying   finishing/folding   ironing

_____ _____ _____ _____ _____ _____ _____

Task 2. Find the words in italics. Then circle the meaning of each word or phrase.

1. When something is *sorted*, it is **classified** / **mixed up** on the basis of any characteristic in common.

53

2. When you check in a very *exclusive* hotel in Swiss, you can enjoy the **high / low** quality service and the very best views of the Swiss Alps right from your hotel room window.

3. When something is *extravagant*, it is **free of charge / very expensive**.

4. When the goods are *distributed*, **the goods are transported /stored** to shops so that they can be sold.

5. When you choose the *dry-clean* service, your laundry is cleaned by using **water / chemicals**.

D Language tip

Bring, take, carry 的用法：

1. 当表示想让某人把某物带给说话人[到这里]时，用 bring。
   例句：I'll bring the towels to your room.

2. 当想让某人把某物带到另一个地方[到那里]时，用 take。
   例句：Jack, please take the towels to Room 1604.

3. 当表示"拿，提，扛"等具有承担重量的含义，[不指明方向性]时，用 carry。
   例句：Will you please carry the box for me?

Choose "bring" "take" or "carry" to complete the sentences.

1. This is Ali Smith from Room 1003, could you _____ me a blanket?

2. Tom, can you _____ a new pillow to Room 1314?

3. Sir, can I help you _____ the luggage?

4. Good afternoon, Mr. White. This is Karen from Housekeeping. Our attendant will _____ some more hangers to your room immediately.

E Test yourself

Task 1. Put the sentences into the right order. The first one has been done for you.

(1) Good morning, sir. I'm the valet to bring the laundry back. Please check your laundry.

(   ) I recommend that you buy a new one back home and send us the receipt. Then we will send you a draft for the amount. What do you think of it?

(   ) But I have to check out and leave. I'm running for an airplane.

(   ) OK, I think so I have to do that.

(   ) Let me have a look. The coat is well washed. But my sweater is out of shape.

(   ) In this case, we are responsible for the damage according to the record on your laundry list. May I know the price of the sweater?

(   ) I'm terribly sorry, sir. May I take it back to the Laundry Department? They may be restore it for you.

(　　) I can't remember it.

(　　) I'm really sorry for the inconvenience cause to you. Thank you for your understanding.

Task 2. Scan the QR code and interpret what you hear from Chinese into English or from English into Chinese.

(1) _____
(2) _____
(3) _____
(4) _____
(5) _____
(6) _____

Activity 2　Acquire Serving Skills

A　The serving skills—basic steps of laundry service attendant

Step one：Receive the guests' requirement for laundry service.

Step two：Collect dirty linens from guestrooms on every hotel floor.

Step three：Send all the dirty linens to the laundry site.

Step four：Sort out the laundry based on their fabric type, color, and stain if there is.

Step five：Wash or dry-clean the dirty linens on guests' requests.

Step six：Fold and iron the clothes on guests' requests.

Step seven：Deliver the laundry back to the guests' room.

B　The guide for guests to use hotel laundry services

1. Separate stained items from the rest of your laundry.
2. Indicate which items need special washing methods.
3. Make sure that your pockets are empty.
4. Sort your laundry.
5. Prepare a bag for your laundry.
6. Confirm the pricing.

C　Special tip

Laundry list is placed in the hotel rooms for guests to enter the details of items they have given for laundry. This list will also feature the price for each laundry item. Laundry list is so important that it will help the hotel and the guest to check the number of items given for laundry and the items which was returned after laundry.

Washington House Inn

LAUNDRY SERVICES   No. 66041

NAME: _____   SIGNATURE: _____

ROOM NO.: _____   DATE: _____

PLEASE TICK✓	PLEASE CALL	PRICE	DELIVERY
☐ Same day service	Before 9am	As listed	By 9pm same day
☐ Same day service	9am-2pm	As listed + 50%	By 9pm same day
☐ Express service	8am-5pm	As listed +100%	Within 5 hours
☐ Next day service	After 9am	As listed	7pm the following day

Please indicate if you wish to be informed of any defects in your garment before cleaning.

☐ Yes   ☐ No

GUEST COUNT	HOTEL COUNT	DESCRIPTION	LAUNDRY PRE ITEM (¥)	TOTAL PRICE (¥)
		Track Suit	¥20.00	
		Trousers/Jeans/Slacks	¥20.00	
		Shirt	¥18.00	
		Blouse	¥18.00	
		T/Sport shirt	¥16.00	
		Dress	¥24.00	
		Skirt	¥18.00	
		Pyjamas	¥14.00	
		Night Gown	¥12.00	
		Shorts	¥10.00	
		Handkerchief	¥4.00	

Conditions of Service		
1. The hotel cannot be held responsible for shrinkage, fastness of colour, or damage resulting from the dry cleaning/pressing process.	BASIC CHARGE	
	EXPRESS SURCHARGE 50% OR 100%	
2. Unless an itemized list is sent, the hotel count must be accepted. Utmost care will be taken to fulfill your requests.	10% SERVICE CHARGE	
3. Please remote all personal belongings from the articles, as the hotel will not be responsible for any loss or damage to articles left in items.	SUBTOTAL	
4. All price quoted are subject to 10% service charge and prevailing government taxes.	GST	
5. DO NOT PAY CASH upon delivery.	GRAND TOTAL	

Activity 3 Practical Training

A Receive the tasks—role play

Task 1. Express Service

Mr. Wang would like to have his suit dry-cleaned. He needs an express service. The attendant explains that the express service takes 4 hours and there is an extra charge of 50%. Mr. Wang has to fill out the laundry list.

Task 2. Delivering the wrong laundry

The valet makes a mistake while sending the laundry back. Mr. Frank can not find his shirt when he checks the returned laundry. The valet makes an apology and promise to find the shirt as soon as possible.

Useful expressions

- I have a suit which needs dry-cleaning.
- The express service takes 4 hours.
- Please fill out the laundry list and sign on it.
- I am the valet to bring the laundry back. May I come in?
- Please check your laundry.
- We are terribly sorry for the inconvenient. We will bring your shirt back as soon as we find it.

B Training card

Name:	Class:	Date:
Your role:	Partner's role:	
Your task:		
Your process:		

(continue)

Conversation between the guest (your partner) and the housemaid (you).

Activity 4   Evaluate Your Study

No.	Tasks	Self-assessment	Group assessment	Teacher evaluation
1	I can tell the main duties of a laundry man on chamber service.			
2	I can read a laundry list.			
3	I can collect the laundry.			
4	I can deliver the laundry to the guest's room.			
5	I can read vocabularies and expressions on chamber service.			

Chinese Story

Chinese Great Figures

There are countless great figures propel China to the forefront of scientific, medicinal, artistic, and philosophical development and lay the foundation for its rich cultural history. They set good examples for us.

Module 2　Housekeeping Department Service客房服务

Yuan Longping（袁隆平）was born in 1930 in Beijing, and graduated from Southwest Agricultural College in 1953. He was one of the greatest agricultural scientist and educator, globally renowned for developing the first hybrid rice strains. Yuan was a hero who will be forever remembered in China and around the world. Dubbed as the "father of hybrid rice", Yuan had devoted his life to the research and development of hybrid rice, and made great contributions to global food security and poverty alleviation.

Tu Youyou（屠呦呦）who was born in 1930, is a Chinese medical scientist, pharmaceutical chemist, and educator. She is best known for discovering artemisinin  (also known as Qinghaosu) and dihydroartemisinin, used to treat malaria, which saved millions of lives. For her discoveries, Tu received the 2015 Nobel Prize for Physiology or Medicine. Tu is the first native Chinese to win Lasker Award in history who was educated in China and whose work was carried out within China.

Chinese people are the creators of history, and they are the real heroes and the source of our strength. Chines people are the fundamental force that determines our country's future.

A. Write down the names and position of the following Chinese sages and great figures.

_____   _____   _____

B. Match the Chinese great people with their strengths or contributions.

Chinese great people	Strengths or contributions
Zhong Nanshan	A forefather of carpenters and architects, inventor of saws and many other carpentry tools.
Fan Jinshi	An educator spending the decades in Yunnan province helping poor, disadvantaged girls to get an education.
Lu Ban	A respiratory expert, on the front line fighting against epidemic diseases.
Zhang Guimei	A great scientist and writer of Great Craft and Inventions.
Confucius	A great scientist and founder of China's missile and space programme.
Song Yingxing	The most famous teacher, philosopher and politician in China, whose ideas have profoundly influenced the civilizations of China.
Qian Xuesen	A leading protector of China's cultural relics, well known as the "Daughter of Dunhuang".
Yang Liwei	A great politician and poet in the Warring States Period, who is the legend of the Dragon Boat Festival.
Qu Yuan	An astronaut, known as "China's first man in space".

C. Work in team.

Do a survey with 4-5 classmates. Select 5 Chinese great figures and list the common qualities from them. If we want to be successful in our future position, what can we learn from them?

Choose a representative from each group to report the result of the survey, and tell your classmates how to do the best job you can.

Module 3: Food and Beverage Department Service
餐饮服务

? Questions for thinking

1. What is the duty of food and beverage department?
2. Do you know what services are provided by food and beverage department in hotels?

Goals

After studying this project, you should be able to:

√ Make reservation for a table or private room.
√ Explain menus, dishes and drinks.
√ Take orders.
√ Know restaurant service procedure.

Prepare for learning

Scan the following QR code to learn the new words and take a test. You can begin the learning of this chapter if your test score is over 70.

扫码听音频

Scene 1 Cooking Methods and Ingredients

Activity 1 Activate Language Knowledge

A Look at the pictures of different items in cuisine, write down the correct vocabulary as quickly as possible

(1) _____ (2) _____ (3) _____ (4) _____

(5) _____ (6) _____ (7) _____ (8) _____

(9) _____ (10) _____ (11) _____ (12) _____

B Scan the QR code and listen to the conversation

扫码听音频

Mary: What are you making? Smells really good!

Tom: I'm making a Chinese dish, braised pork belly.

Mary: Pork belly? Sounds interesting.

Tom: Yes, it tastes very good. Very flavorful, very tender, but not greasy.

Mary: Wow, how do you make it?

Tom: Well, very simple, all you need for ingredients are pork belly, ginger, spring onion, soy sauce, sugar and salt.

Mary: So you just put everything into the pot?

Tom: No, you need to seal the meat first with hot oil in a pan, then add all the seasonings and add water just above the surface of the meat. Let it simmer for 20 minutes, and it's done!

Mary: Sounds not very difficult.
Tom: Not at all, go try it out yourself.
Mary: OK! I definitely will.

Task 1. Discussion with classmates

1. What dish is Tom making?
2. What ingredients are used for braised pork belly?
3. How much water should be used?

Task 2. Practice with teammates

Match the following words with teammates:

(1) 红烧　　　　　(A) Stir-fry
(2) 蒸　　　　　　(B) Pan-fry
(3) 炒　　　　　　(C) Steam
(4) 炸　　　　　　(D) Deep-fry
(5) 煎　　　　　　(E) Roast
(6) 烤　　　　　　(F) Braise

C Read the passage on cuisine.

We all love take-out food, but home-cooked meals are actually the easiest way to improve your health, and to cut down your grocery budget.

扫码听音频

Whether you live by yourself or with family, to prepare home-cooked meals always seems like a difficult task, too busy to find the time and energy. Eating out or ordering in are the fastest, simplest option.

Frozen food like pizza, or other pre-made meals, as well as instant noodles, instant rice, self-heating food, are usually high in chemical additives, sugar, salt, unhealthy fat, and calories.

Many restaurants serve portions that are twice bigger than the recommended dietary guidelines. This encourages you to eat more than you would at home.

Note

grocery　*n.* 食品杂货

chemical additive *n.* 化学添加剂
calorie　*n.* 卡路里(热量单位)

You will have more control over the ingredients and portion size when you prepare your own meals. A healthy eating habit can be made by using less sugar, salt and transfats. Use variety of protein foods such as seafood, lean meats and poultry, eggs, beans and peas, nuts and seeds. Consume more vegetables and fruits. By cooking for yourself, you can ensure that you and your family eat fresh, wholesome meals.

Cooking at home helps you to build better knowledge on nutrition.

protein	n.	蛋白质
wholesome	adj.	有益健康的
nutrition	n.	营养

Decide whether the statements are true(T) or false(F) after reading.

(　　) 1. You can eat instant food on a regular basis.
(　　) 2. Restaurant serves small portion meals, that's why it's more costly eating out.
(　　) 3. Beans and peas are high in protein.
(　　) 4. Cooking at home is a time-consuming task. That is why people like to eat out.

D Language tip

Basic knife cuts

cut：v. 切，表达所有"切"的动作。
　　　例句：Wash and cut the carrot. 把胡萝卜洗净切了。
chop：v. 切碎，剁碎，砍。
　　　例句：Add the finely chopped celery. 加入切碎的西芹。
slice：n. 片，A slice of bread. 一片面包。
　　　v. 把…切成薄片 He sliced the onion. 他把洋葱切了片。
dice：v. 切成丁，切成小方块。
　　　例句：She diced the potato for soup. 她把土豆切丁做汤。
mince：v. 切碎（细碎），用机器绞（肉）。
　　　例句：He minced the pork. 他把猪肉搅成馅。 Minced garlic. 蒜蓉。
shred：v. 切碎（成条），撕碎。
　　　例句：Shredded chicken breast is great for cold noodle. 鸡胸肉丝用来做凉面特别好。
peel：v. 削皮，剥皮。
　　　例句：My mom showed me how to peel an apple. 我妈妈教我怎么削苹果。

Choose the correct verbs to complete the dialogue.

　　　　　　　　　　mince　　cut　　shred　　slice

Knowing basic knife cuts makes you one step closer to a good cook. To make homemade hamburger, first you need to _____ the sesame bun into two pieces. Before getting your grill ready, _____ the beef, or just buy some ground beef to make burger patty. _____ some onions and tomatoes into very thin circles. _____ some lettuces into big pieces. Then grill the beef patty, toast the bread. Finally layer all ingredients into a sandwich, add ketchup, cheese and pickle, yum!

E Test yourself

Task 1. Put the following sentences into the right order. The first one has been done for you.

(1) I'm planning for making a big New Year dinner.
(   ) What a big meal. What kind of dumpling are you making?
(   ) What are you making exactly?
(   ) OK.
(   ) That's nice, I know you are a good cook.
(   ) I haven't decided yet. Maybe leek with pork or cabbage with shrimp.
(   ) I'm going to make BBQ pork, roasted chicken, steamed fish, stir-fry string beans, dumplings, and sweet & sour soup.

Task 2. Scan the QR code and interpret what you hear from Chinese into English or from English into Chinese.

(1) _____
(2) _____
(3) _____
(4) _____
(5) _____
(6) _____

Activity 2   Chinese Dish Translation

A Translation principles based on ingredients

1. 以食材为主
主料+with+辅料。例如，Beef with bitter melon 苦瓜炒牛肉。
2. 以烹饪法为主
烹饪法+主料。例如，Roasted chicken 烤鸡。
烹饪法+主料+with+辅料。例如，Stir-fry pork with string beans 豆角炒肉。
烹饪法+主料+with/in+汤汁。例如，Braised beef with brown sauce 红烧牛肉；Steamed chicken in chili sauce 口水鸡。

B Translation principles based on taste and texture or origin:

1. 以口感为主

   口感+主料。例如，Crispy fried spare ribs 香酥排骨。

2. 以人名、地名为主

   人名、地名+主料。例如，Mapo Tofu 麻婆豆腐、Beijing roasted duck 北京烤鸭。

C Special tip

When describing a dish with different ingredients and sauce, the most appropriate prepositions are "in" and "with".

Here are the rules for it.

> ☆介词 in 和 with 在汤汁、配料中的用法
>
> 1. 主料是浸在汤汁或配料中时，使用 in 连接。
>
>   例如，Steamed beef ribs **in** black pepper sauce. 黑椒牛仔骨。
>
> 2. 汤汁或蘸料和主料是分开的，或是后浇在主菜上的，则用 **with** 连接。
>
>   例如，Japanese noodle soup **with** seafood. 海鲜乌冬汤面。

Activity 3   Practical Training

A Receive the tasks—role play

Task 1. Recommend food

John goes to a restaurant for a meal as soon as he arrived in China, hoping that the waiter could help to recommend authentic Guangzhou cuisine.

Task 2. Recipe of favourite dish

You and your classmates try to discuss and write your own recipe of favorite dish according to following sample.

Sample：

Shrimp Fried Rice
Ingredients： 　　1 bowl of cooked white rice 　　50 g shrimp 　　2 eggs 　　20 g onion 　　5 g green onion

Module 3 Food and Beverage Department Service 餐饮服务

(continue)

	Shrimp Fried Rice
	Preparation: 1. Whisk the eggs, add 1/3 teaspoon of salt. 2. Chop the onion, green onion into fine dice. 3. Place 40 g of oil into a pan and heat over medium high heat. 4. Stir in the egg and cook until firm, then remove eggs from the pan, and set aside. 5. Add 5 g of oil into pan, add onion, cook until it is transparent, then add rice, stir and cook for 5 mins. 6. Add 1/3 teaspoon of salt.
	Ingredients: ***Preparation***:

Useful expressions

- What dish are you making?
- My favorite food is Mexican food.
- What are the ingredients?
- What tables do you like?
- I'm sorry, the restaurant is full.
- We look forward to having you with us.

B Training card

Name:	Class:		Date:
Your role:		Partner's role:	
Your task:			

(continue)

Your process:

Conversation between the guest (your partner) and the reservationist (you).

🏃 Activity 4　Evaluate Your Study

No.	Tasks	Self-assessment	Group assessment	Teacher evaluation
1	I can tell the basic knife cuts.			
2	I can tell the cooking methods.			
3	I know how to translate Chinese dishes into English properly.			
4	I can write my own recipe.			
5	I can master vocabularies and expressions on cooking methods and ingredients.			

Module 3 Food and Beverage Department Service 餐饮服务

Scene 2 Service During the Meal(1)

Activity 1 Activate Language Knowledge

A Look at the pictures of different types of seats in restaurant, write down the correct vocabulary or phrase as quickly as possible

(1) _____ (2) _____ (3) _____ (4) _____

(5) _____ (6) _____ (7) _____ (8) _____

B Scan the QR code and listen to the conversation

扫码听音频

Reservationist: John's restaurants, how may I help you?
Guest: Hello, I would like to make a table reservation for tomorrow night.
Reservationist: Sure, may I have your name please?
Guest: Mike Xu.
Reservationist: Great, Mr. Xu, what time will you be arriving?
Guest: 7:30 pm.
Reservationist: OK, and for how many persons?
Guest: 3, there will be 2 adults and 1 child.
Reservationist: Sure, no problem, we do have seats available. Do you have any preferences?
Guest: I'm not sure, it will be my first visit.
Reservationist: We have nice window seats, with a good view over the city center.
Guest: OK, sounds good. Thanks for your suggestion. I also need a child's booster seat please.
Reservationist: No problem, Mr. Xu, I'll note it down. Can I have your phone number please?
Guest: 130 **** 1236.
Reservationist: A table for three at 7:30 pm, by the window, with a child's booster seat, for Mr. Mike Xu. Phone number is 130 **** 389.

Guest: That's right.

Reservationist: Thank you, Mr. Xu, your reservation has been made. If you have any further questions, or would like to make any changes, please don't hesitate to contact us.

Guest: OK, thanks.

Reservationist: Thank you very much for your call. Have a great day.

Task 1. Discussion with classmates

1. What information should be collected to make a restaurant reservation.
2. Have you notice how many times does the reservationist greet the guest by name? Why is it important?
3. Why does reservationist need to ask guest's preferences?

Task 2. Practice with teammates

Write down the sequence of make a table reservation?
(1) guest's name   (2) guest's phone number/room number
(3) number of persons   (4) time of arrival
(5) preference of seats

C Read the passage on restaurant reservation

You may wonder why we need to make a reservation before heading to restaurants. In order for restaurant owners to keep organized, maximize table turnover, and reduce waiting time for customers, it's important to keep reservation well organized.

Restaurant reservations first began with managers, hostesses, or other staff taking phone calls and penciling in names and times on paper. This took away a lot of time from hostesses and other staff members who could be clearing tables or helping customers. However, as technology advances, and more and more people have constant access to the internet, companies have developed various restaurant reservation software to make the process quicker and more convenient for both the restaurant staff and custom-

Note

turnover	n. 周转率，营业额
hostess	n. 迎宾女招待
access	n. 通道，使用权 v. 访问，使用
various	adj. 各种各样的

ers. Restaurants can either create its own website for on-line booking, there are many third-party reservation services available as well, depending on restaurant location, staff and traffic.

Another point for restaurant owner to setup their online reservation system is that, online reservation system allows convenient 24/7 access, not only during restaurant operating hours. Customers don't need to call and wait for an employee to answer. Less incorrect information will be collected, since everything will be typed in by customers directly.

third-party	*n.* 第三方
type	*v.* 打字

Decide whether the statements are true(T) or false(F) after reading.

(   ) 1. Customers prefer the traditional way of booking a table.
(   ) 2. Reservation is to help a restaurant serve more guests.
(   ) 3. Hostess is someone who welcomes guests and leads the way.
(   ) 4. Online reservation system will collect only correct information.

D Language tip

日期英文的表述

1. 月份用英文拼写或公认简写

   例如，Jan.—January; Feb.—February; Mar.—March。

   注意：五月(May)没有缩写。

2. 数字可用序数词或基数词

   例如，1st; 2nd; 3rd; 4th; 5th 或 1, 2, 3, 4, 5。

3. 日期书写顺序

   1)月日年

   例如，August 15th, 2001 或 August 15, 2001。

   2)日月年

   例如，15th August, 2001 或 15 August, 2001。

4. 日期读法

   要在日期前加the，数字要读序数词

   例如，2001年8月15日。

   The fifteenth **of** August, two thousand and one.

   August **the** fifteenth, two thousand and one.

Translate the following into English.

1. 2015年6月18日 _____
2. 1993年9月22日 _____
3. 2023年1月31日 _____

E Test yourself

Task 1. Put the sentences into the right order. The first one has been done for you.

(1) Good evening, Michael's steak house, how can I help you?

(   ) Well, not even one small table in the corner?

(   ) Very good, Mr. Martin, one table for 3, on the day after tomorrow at 7:30 pm.

(   ) I'm very sorry that all tables are booked for tomorrow evening.

(   ) Chris Martin, 130 **** 1121.

(   ) I'm sorry but no. We do have one table available at lunch time tomorrow, would you like to do that?

(   ) Lunch time…I'm not sure. What else do you have?

(   ) OK, sir, can I have your name and phone number please?

(   ) Alright, I guess I'll have to make it for 7:30 pm, the day after tomorrow.

(   ) I want to book a table for three for tomorrow night.

(   ) We will be less busy on the day after tomorrow.

(   ) That's right.

(   ) Thank you for your call. Have a great day.

Task 2. Scan the QR code and interpret what you hear from Chinese into English or from English into Chinese.

(1) _____

(2) _____

(3) _____

(4) _____

(5) _____

(6) _____

扫码听音频

Activity 2   Acquire Serving Skills

A The serving skills—table reservation procedure

Step one: Greet the guests.

Step two: Ask whether the guests want a private room or not.

Step three: Ask information of table reservation: time of arrival and number of people.

Step four: Check availability.

Step five: Ask special demands.

Step six: Ask name and contact information.

Step seven: Confirm.

Step eight: Express your expectation to the guests.

B The details when do the table reservation

1. Pay more attention to the demand on private room.

2. Don't forget to ask seat preferences—if the guests like window seats, booth or quiet corner.

3. Make sure to ask if there will be infants or children. Provide necessary care.

4. Be sure to take down guest's name and phone number.

5. Always confirm at the end.

C Special tip

1. Reject your guests politely. Don't reject guests directly, always give other alternatives. For example, restaurant tables are fully booked, ask the guests if they want to come some other time, give clear time and dates information.

2. Always call your guests by their last name. It is a sign of respect. Very important to do that if you want to impress your customers.

Activity 3   Practical Training

A Receive the tasks—role play

Task 1. Changing reservation

Michael has made a reservation for 3 people on 3rd April, at 7:30 pm, now he wants to make changes to the reservation. He asks if he can come early at 6:30 pm.

Restaurant do have table available for him.

Task 2. Canceling reservation

Chris has other plans for the weekend, he has a reservation for brunch in Hotel Sofitel on 22nd May, now he wants to cancel the reservation.

Useful expressions

- How may I assist you today?
- Sorry to have kept you waiting.
- One minute please. I'll check it for you.
- What tables do you like?
- I'm sorry, the restaurant is full.
- We look forward to having you with us.

B Training card

Name:	Class:	Date:

Your role: Partner's role:

Your task:

Your process:

Conversation between the guest (your partner) and the reservationist (you).

Activity 4   Evaluate Your Study

No.	Tasks	Self-assessment	Group assessment	Teacher evaluation
1	I can tell the procedure of making a table reservation.			

Module 3 Food and Beverage Department Service 餐饮服务

(continue)

No.	Tasks	Self-assessment	Group assessment	Teacher evaluation
2	I know how to reject guests politely.			
3	I know how to take a reservation properly.			
4	I can make changes to a reservation.			
5	I can master vocabularies and expressions on restaurant reservation.			

Scene 3   Service During the Meal(2)

Activity 1   Activate Language Knowledge

A Look at the pictures of different items in restaurant, write down the correct vocabulary or phrase as quickly as possible

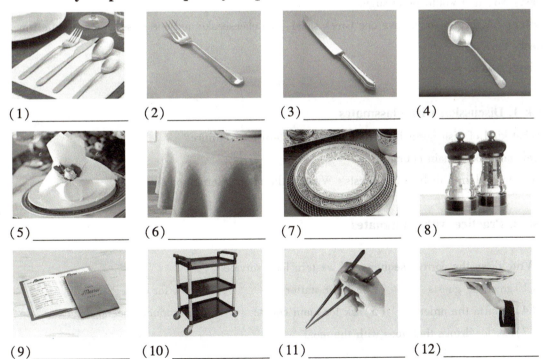

(1)_____   (2)_____   (3)_____   (4)_____

(5)_____   (6)_____   (7)_____   (8)_____

(9)_____   (10)_____ (11)_____ (12)_____

B Scan the QR code and listen to the conversation

Waiter: Good evening, here is our menu madam, please have look.

Guest: Thank you.

Waiter: Our special of the day is T-bone steak, served with French fries, and black pepper sauce. Please take your time, I'll be back in few minutes. (*A few moments later……*)

Waiter: May I take your order now?

Guest: Yes.

Waiter: Any starter to begin with?

Guest: Yes, but can you explain what a Greek salad is?

Waiter: Absolutely, Greek salad is made with cucumber, bell pepper, red onion, cherry tomato, and some feta cheese. It's a very fresh and crispy salad.

Guest: Feta cheese, sounds very good, then I'll try that.

Waiter: Very good choice, and for your main course?

Guest: I'll skip the main course.

Waiter: OK, no problem. You want to decide your dessert now or later?

Guest: I can order it now. One cheesecake would be fine.

Waiter: Would you like anything to drink?

Guest: One glass of house white wine should be good.

Waiter: Would you like anything else?

Guest: No, that would be enough.

Waiter: Alright, so you'll have one Greek salad, one cheesecake and one glass of house white wine.

Guest: Correct.

Waiter: Thank you.

Task 1. Discussion with classmates

1. What kind of dish normally served first in western food culture?
2. Can salad be a main course?
3. How to explain a dish to the guests? What is the main information?

Task 2. Practice with teammates

Write down the correct sequence of western food service.

(1) greet the guests   (2) ask for starter   (3) ask for dessert

(4) confirm the order   (5) ask for main course   (6) introduce special dishes

(7) ask for drinks that goes with the meal

Module 3 Food and Beverage Department Service 餐饮服务

C Read the passage on restaurant service

A waiter or waitress is a person whose job is to serve customers in restaurants, bars, and other food serving and drinking places. They make sure the guests have a wonderful *dining* experience. Being a good waiter or waitress not only has to deliver foods and drinks to the table. Knowing how to make *appropriate* menu recommendations is important. Right food selection can increase satisfaction to the guests, also increases restaurant *revenue*.

扫码听音频

The right waiter/waitress uplifts the dining experience for customers. Hiring a *responsible* individual is not easy. Being a good server is not easy neither. Restaurants are relying on someone who has the patience to all questions and unique requests from customers. Good waiter/waitress should be able to handle *chores* in fast-paced environment, being an expert on multi-tasking, and also be able to effectively communicate with kitchen or bar staffs to deliver orders accurately and promptly. Communication skills are a staple of every job advertisement. Waiting will improve one's social skills and communication skills to the next level.

Working as a waiter can get a bigger picture of the business and gain a set of useful skills that can one day be applied in other jobs.

Note		
dining	*n.*	用餐
appropriate	*adj.*	合适的、相称的
revenue	*n.*	收入
responsible	*adj.*	负责的
chore	*n.*	杂务、琐事

Decide whether the statements are true(T) or false(F) after reading.

(　　) 1. A waiter or waitress should make sure the guests have a wonderful dining experience.

(　　) 2. It is not important to make appropriate menu recommendations to the guests as a waiter or waitress.

(　　) 3. Restaurants are relying on waiters or waitresses who have the patience to all questions and unique requests from customers.

(　　) 4. A waiter or waitress can grasp main points of the business and learn lots of skills.

D Language tip

Can, could, may 的区别:

1. 三者为均情态动词,都可以用来发出请求和许可的建议,可用于疑问句。

例句：**Can** I borrow your book？我能借用你的书吗？

Could I borrow your book？我可以借用你的书吗？

May I borrow your book？能允许我借用你的书吗？

2. 当提出请求，表示征求对方意见和允许时，may 是最正式的，could 比 can 更为礼貌，Can 是最简单直接的表达。

3. 注意：may 只能接 I，可以说 may I，但不能说 may you。

4. 在正式的场合和面对不熟悉的人，尤其在酒店业、服务业中，为体现职业性和尊重客人，一般用 could 和 may。

Choose the best verbs to complete the sentences.

        can   could   may

1. _____ you open the window for me please?
2. _____ I take a photo for you?
3. _____ I unfold the napkin for you?
4. _____ you show me the way?
5. _____ I have a cup of tea, please?

E Test yourself

Task 1. Put the sentences into the right order. The first one has been done for you

(1) Good evening, Are you ready to order?

( ) I don't quite understand the menu, And I don't know anything about Chinese food.

( ) That's nice, I'll have that!

( ) OK, What do you recommend?

( ) Two dishes would be enough for you. Would you also want to try some soup?

( ) Do you like spicy food?

( ) No, I don't eat spicy food.

( ) I'm allergic to crab, But I can eat other seafoods like fish and shrimp.

( ) No worries, I can give you some good advice.

( ) I suggest you have our famous steamed fish with light soy sauce. Fishes are caught daily from our local harbor.

( ) Alright, We also have a very nice traditional dish, sweet and sour pork spear ribs.

( ) Sound good! I love sweet and sour dishes.

( ) No, I don't like soup, especially in the summer.

( ) Thank you.

( ) Or maybe you can have something to drink?

( ) OK, I'll have an apple juice.

( ) So, one steamed fish with light soy sauce, one sweet and sour pork spear ribs and one apple juice.

( ) Your dishes are coming right up.

( ) Alright, no problem, do you prefer to try some of our seafood?

Task 2. Scan the QR code and interpret what you hear from Chinese into English or from English into Chinese.

扫码听音频

(1) _____
(2) _____
(3) _____
(4) _____
(5) _____
(6) _____

Activity 2 Acquire Serving Skills

A The serving skills—western food service procedure

Step one: Greet the guests, present menu properly.

Step two: Unfold napkins for the guests, ask if they like to have something to drink.

Step three: Give the bread and water.

Step four: Take the order.

Step five: Provide recommendations on food and wine.

Step six: Repeat the order.

Step seven: First serve for appetizer or starter, soup, then main course, lastly dessert.

Step eight: Give the bill.

Step nine: Show appreciation.

B The details in restaurant service

1. Always remember "lady first".
2. Always ask if guests have any food allergies.
3. Most commonly, food and drinks are served and cleared from the guests' right side.
4. Cutleries must be provided according to the dish.

   Starter is usually given small table fork and knife.

   Soup is given soup spoon.

   Main course is given big table fork and knife.

   Steak is given steak knife.

Fish is given fish fork and knife.

Dessert is given small tablespoon and fork.

5. Wine mush be served in wine glasses.
6. Red wine must be served in room temperature, white and rose wine must be served chilled.

C Special tip

When it comes to beef steak cooking, here are five types of steak cooking levels. It is very important to ask your guests how they like their steak cooked.

rare	一分熟
medium rare	三分熟
medium	五分熟
medium well	七分熟
well done	全熟

Activity 3   Practical Training

A Receive the tasks—role play

Task 1. Restaurant service

Mr. and Mrs. Zhang go to an Italian restaurant, they don't have any reservation, and they would like to sit by the window. Waiter Jessica receives them, she recommends dishes. The guests order beef steak.

Task 2. Room service

A guest calls hotel restaurant to order room service. Waiter takes the order and records special demands. The guest wants extra cheese on the salad, extra ice in sparkling water. Food needs to be delivered as soon as possible.

Useful expressions

- Here is our menu.
- Are you ready to order? / Have you made your decision?
- How would you like your steak?
- What is the special of the day?
- It comes with…
- May I suggest…

Module 3　Food and Beverage Department Service 餐饮服务

B　Training card

Name:	Class:	Date:
Your role:		Partner's role:
Your task:		
Your process:		

Conversation between the guest (your partner) and the waiter (you).

Activity 4　Evaluate Your Study

No.	Tasks	Self-assessment	Group assessment	Teacher evaluation
1	I can present menu properly.			
2	I can tell the procedure of order taking.			
3	I can make recommendations on food.			
4	I can tell the details of Western cuisine service.			
5	I can master vocabularies and expressions on restaurant service.			

Scene 4　　　　Beverage Service

Activity 1　　Activate Language Knowledge

A Look at the pictures of different items in restaurant and bar, write down the correct vocabulary or phrase as quickly as possible

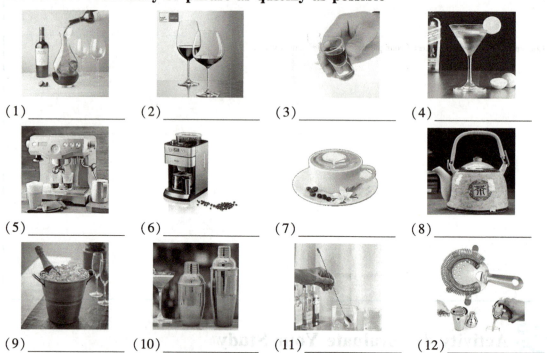

(1) _____　　(2) _____　　(3) _____　　(4) _____

(5) _____　　(6) _____　　(7) _____　　(8) _____

(9) _____　　(10) _____　　(11) _____　　(12) _____

B Scan the QR code and listen to the conversation

扫码听音频

Waiter: Good evening. Can I get you anything to drink?

Guest: Yes, but I need to look through the drink list first. Give me a moment.

Waiter: Absolutely madam, take as long as you need. Do you need any recommendation?

Guest: Do you have any non-alcoholic beverage?

Waiter: Yes, we do have a few very nice options. If you like classic cocktails, such as Mojito and Pina Colada, we have the non-alcoholic version.

Guest: Emmm…… I'm not a big fan of mixed drinks. Do you have any juice?

Waiter: Sure, we have fresh pressed juice, like apple juice, orange juice, lime juice and grapefruit juice.

Guest: Grapefruit juice would be fine.

Waiter: Would you like it chilled or at room temperature?

Guest: Can I have it with extra ice please.

Waiter: Yes, very good, one grapefruit juice with extra ice. Just a moment, please.

Task 1. Discussion with classmates

1. How to explain a drink to a guest, what information should be given?
2. Do you think selling skill is important in order taking? How to do it?
3. Excellent service is very detail oriented, have you notice any detailed service from the dialogue?

Task 2. Practice with teammates

Make a list of beverage categories on a drink list:

1.
2.
3.
4.
5.
…

C Read the passage on restaurant beverage service

Beverage service is an important part of F&B service. It is one of the most profitable business which has drawn many investor's attention. Professional beverage service requires years of training, practice and knowledge. There are many different types of beverage service that is provided in hotels, restaurants, tea shops, coffee shops, and the most common, bars. Although the basic method is quite similar, there are some differences. Four different types of beverage services are as follow:

1. Counter service. Bartenders work behind the counter, guests usually standing or seating at the bar counter for consuming the drink. The bartenders will take orders and prepare drinks in front of the guests. It requires excellent

扫码听音频

Note

investor   n. 投资者

counter   n. 柜台
bartender   n. 调酒师、
              酒吧侍者

bartending skills and communication skills.

2. Tray service. Amount all beverage service, tray service is the simplest type of all beverage service. The main duty of this job is to carry ready drinks from the bar to the guests by using trays. Usually this happens in stand-up cocktail reception where there are no tables.

3. Velvet service. It is also called as "club service", which is the highest level of beverage service. It can be found in fine dining restaurants, hotel lounges and clubs. Service is focused very much on details; drinks are made upon request.

4. Bottle sale service. It is commonly served in lounges, night-clubs and pubs. The service procedures are quite similar to Velvet service, except the spirits are sold by bottles. Ice are served in ice bucket with tongs along with the bottle. Customers choose to serve by themselves, and they will be given a card for further visit, if the bottle is not finished.

cocktail reception	n. 鸡尾酒会
velvet	n. 天鹅绒
fine dining	n. 精致餐饮、雅宴
spirit	n. 烈酒

Decide whether the statements are true(T) or false(F) after reading.

(　　) 1. Owning a bar does not make much money.
(　　) 2. Bartender usually needs to work years to reach professional level.
(　　) 3. Tray service required high communication and bartending skills.
(　　) 4. The name "velvet" represents quantity of service.

D Language tip

So, too, neither, either 的用法：

1. I like Thai food a lot.
   So do I. / I do, **too**.
2. She is crazy about playing chess.
   So am I. / I am, **too**.
3. My child can eat really spicy food.
   So can I. / I can, **too**.

4. I don't like greasy food.
   Neither do I. / I don't, **either**.
5. She is not interested in Indian movie.
   Neither am I. / I'm not **either**.
6. My child can not stand dessert.
   Neither can I. / I can't **either**.

Give your responses to these statements.

1. I like the weather in Guangzhou.

Chinese Story

Chinese Tea Culture

Tea is a part of people's everyday life in China. Chinese people love tea as Western people love coffee. In China, tea culture is not all about drinking tea. It is actually an art of brewing tea, appreciating tea, smelling tea, and tasting tea. Many families drink tea after meal or when treating guests. It is not only a healthy habit but also represents rich culture and tradition. Tea is a symbol of great hospitality. Chinese people can chat with a friend for a whole afternoon over a pot of good tea.

True Chinese tea lovers will not accept store-bought tea bags. Chinese tea preparation required new tea leaves, spring water, clean tea sets and people with good manners. To brew a good cup of tea is to learn how to keep the balance of method, water, temperature and time. However, tea brewing techniques varies based on different types of tea, and good water source is always the key.

To drink tea could be consider as a way to connecting to the nature and to better appreciate life. Tea tasting has cultural meaning. For traditional tea tasting, tea must match surrounding elements such as cool wind, moon light, pine, bamboo, plum blossom and snow. All these show the ultimate goal of Chinese culture: the harmonious unity of human beings with nature.

A. Complete the table with the given information. the name of main categories of tea in Chinese and match the fermentation level

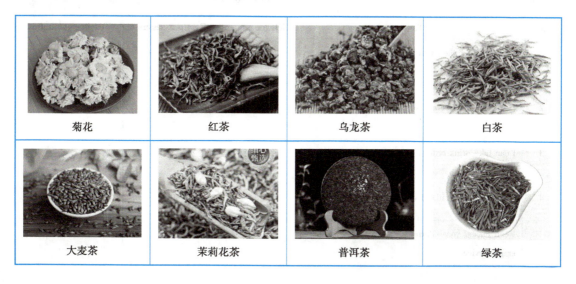

Module 3　Food and Beverage Department Service 餐饮服务

- Would you like some wine with your……(dish)?
- It is a sweet /sour/ dry/ bitter drink.
- This……(drink) goes very well with……(dish). Would you like to try it?

B Training card

Name:	Class:	Date:
Your role:	Partner's role:	
Your task:		
Your process:		
Conversation between the guest (your partner) and the waiter (you).		

Activity 4　Evaluate Your Study

No.	Tasks	Self-assessment	Group assessment	Teacher evaluation
1	I can explain the main characteristics of Chinese alcoholic beverage.			
2	I can tell the beverage service procedure.			
3	I can take drink orders.			
4	I can tell the details of wine service.			
5	I can master vocabularies and expressions on beverage service.			

B The details when serving wine

1. Wine is served from the right side of the guests.
2. Wine bottle should never touch the glass when pouring.
3. Wine bottle foil caps should be removed before opening the bottle.
4. Wine decanter is not always necessary.
5. Never fill the wine glass to the top. Generally, the standard is about 150mL per serving in Western food service. In Chinese food service, 80% of a glassful is right.
6. Always face the wine label to the guests.

C Special tip

There are many different categories of wines, or alcohols related to wine. Most commonly are red wine, white wine, rose wine, champagne (sparkling wine), brandy, port, sherry and vermouth.

Table wine is for daily drinking and paring wine with food dishes can enhance the dinning experience. Here are some wine and food matching guide.

1. Red wine with red meat; goes well with steak, roasted meat dish and pasta.
2. White wine with white (light) meat; goes well with chicken, fish and seafood, and salad or cold meat dishes.

Activity 3 Practical Training

A Receive the tasks—role play

Task 1. Recommendation in a bar

A guest is ordering drinks in a bar, he likes sweet and fruity drinks and asks for recommendations. Waiter first asks for taste preference, then makes a recommendation and takes the order.

Task 2. Recommendation in a restaurant

A guest is having dinner in an Italian restaurant, he has ordered a seafood spaghetti, waiter make wine recommendation based on the food.

Useful expressions

- Here is the drink list, please take your time.
- What kind of drinks do you like?

Module 3 Food and Beverage Department Service 餐饮服务

2. I can eat any kind of food. _____
3. Jack does not enjoy the rich food very much. _____
4. Monica thinks Mexican food is delicious. _____
5. This boy can not stand reading books. _____
6. I don't like going shopping with my mom. _____

E Test yourself

Task 1. Put the sentences into the right order. The first one has been done for you.

(1) Welcome to our bar, do you have a reservation?
(   ) Cool! That's exactly what I like, I'll have that.
(   ) What is this "Alexander"?
(   ) Alright Ms. Du, this way please. Here is our drink list, please take your time.
(   ) It is a very classic cognac-based cocktail. It consists of equal parts of cognac, cream and brown cacao liqueur. It's creamy and sweet.
(   ) Wonderful, one Alexander coming right up.
(   ) Yes, it's under Christina Du, Room 3012.

Task 2. Scan the QR code and interpret what you hear from Chinese into English or from English into Chinese.

扫码听音频

(1) _____
(2) _____
(3) _____
(4) _____
(5) _____
(6) _____

Activity 2 Acquire Serving Skills

A The serving skills—wine service procedure

When doing wine service, it is important to know the correct procedure.

Step one: Take wine order. Make sure to confirm the producer, grape types and year.
Step two: Check the bottle before serving: label, information, cleanness, temperature.
Step three: Show the bottle with label facing to the guests, repeat the wine information.
Step four: Ask for permission then open the bottle.
Step five: Ask the guests who has made the order to taste the wine.
Step six: Serve the rest of guests on the table, lastly serve the one who has tasted the wine.

Module 3 Food and Beverage Department Service 餐饮服务

The fermentation level:

unfermented   lightly fermented   half fermented   fully fermented   post fermented

Tea/Herbal tea	Chinese translation	Picture	Fermentation level
White tea			
Green tea			
Oolong tea			
Black tea			
Pu-erh			
Jasmine			
Chrysanthemum flower			
Barley tea			

B. Work in pairs. Discuss the occasion when people need to drink or offer tea

1. _____
2. _____
3. _____
4. _____

C. Work in team.

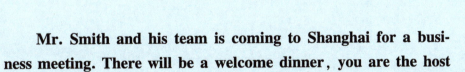

Mr. Smith and his team is coming to Shanghai for a business meeting. There will be a welcome dinner, you are the host of this event, please chose three type of Chinese tea.

②

Choose a representative from each group to explain to your guests how to prepare the tea you have chosen. Show what is traditional Chinese tea etiquette.

Module 4

Concierge
礼宾

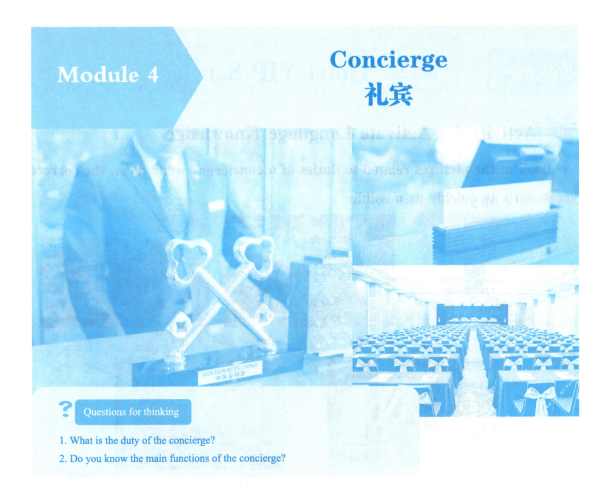

? Questions for thinking

1. What is the duty of the concierge?
2. Do you know the main functions of the concierge?

Goals

After studying this project, you should be able to:
- √ Deal with VIP reception.
- √ Provide meeting services.
- √ Give sightseeing suggestions.
- √ Know concierge working procedure.
- √ Understand how to fill the Cash Flow Statement.

Prepare for learning

Scan the following QR code to learn the new words and take a test.

扫码听音频

酒店英语

Scene 1　　　Hotel VIP Service

Activity 1　Activate Language Knowledge

A Look at the pictures related to duties of a concierge, write down the correct vocabulary as quickly as possible

(1) _____　　(2) _____　　(3) _____

(4) _____　　(5) _____

(6) _____　　(7) _____

B Scan the QR code and listen to the conversations

扫码听音频

Concierge: Good morning, madam. Welcome to the Grand Hotel. I am Richard, and I'll escort you to your room.
Guest: Thanks a lot.
Concierge: Come this way, please. We'll take Elevator 2.
Guest: Alright. What kinds of restaurants do you have here, by the way?
Concierge: We have three Chinese ones, a western one, and a Japanese one. And we also have a mini bar and a 24-hour coffee shop. Here's the elevator. After you, madam.

(*After a while*)

Guest: Oh, what a lovely room.

Concierge: We're glad that you like it, madam. Would you like me to introduce the VIP amenities to you?

Guest: Yes, please.

Concierge: Our hotel is a five-star one. Everything you might need can be found here, from a personal working desk with iMac desktop and complimentary WiFi internet, to a satellite TV. You can also relax in your private garden, or enjoy dinner at your private outdoor lounge.

Guest: This sounds amazing!

Concierge: Should you have any other requests, please let us know. Hope you have a pleasant stay in our hotel.

Task 1. Discussion with classmates

1. What kinds of details need to be checked when blocking the room for a VIP guest?
2. What do you do upon a VIP guest's arrival?
3. How do you deal with an unexpected VIP guest?

Task 2. Practice with teammates

1. Who can provide concierge service? Please tick the box(es).

(1) courier ☐   (2) doorman ☐
(3) porter ☐   (4) airport representative ☐
(5) housekeeper ☐   (6) housekeeper ☐

C Read the passage on the working procedure of concierges

扫码听音频

The Merriam-Webster Dictionary generally defines "concierge" as a French word, meaning "gatekeeper" or "keeper of the keys". The position has its origin going back to the time of palaces and castles in ancient France. The royal household employed a concierge whose job was to cater to the needs of VIP visitors as well as to hold the keys to many castle rooms.

Note

gatekeeper *n.* 看门人，门卫

cater to 迎合，为……服务

The basic duties of concierges are to provide the bell service and attend to guests' needs. They serve guests in the room, in the lobby, and in other public areas, run errands, and assist at departure. On the guest's arrival, the bellman carries his/her luggage from the car. The luggage stays on the lobby floor until the guest finishes registering. With the room slip at hand, the bellman escorts the guest with his or her luggage to the room. Once inside the room, the bellman performs the inspection function, checking the lights and other facilities, explaining some special features of the hotel, and pointing out the self-service items.

Besides the bell service, concierges must be knowledgeable about the surrounding community, including the hotel itself. Typically, they provide directions and information on local attractions and facilities, as well as arranging for airplane, theater or other reservations.

bell service		应接服务
lobby	n.	大厅，大堂
departure	n.	离开
room slip		配房通知单
inspection	n.	检查
knowledgeable	adj.	有见识的

Decide whether the statements are true(T) or false(F) after reading.

(　　) 1. Concierges should provide their service throughout the whole process.
(　　) 2. Concierges should lead guests to their rooms.
(　　) 3. Concierges should check the facilities and supplies in the room.
(　　) 4. Concierges should have extensive working experiences.

D Language tip

分词形容词(**participles as adjectives**)是形容词的一个主要子类，用来描述感觉或者反应。

现在分词：动词+ing
表达修饰词给人的感受或主动的动作。
This new book is fascinating.
The students can't answer the confusing question.

过去分词：动词+ed
表达修饰词本身的感受或被加诸的动作
I'm fascinated by this new book.
The confused students can't answer the question.

Complete the short passage below with the correct form of these words.

amaze　　annoy　　bore　　disgust　　embarrass　　shock

Joey had a terrible time at the football match. First, his ticket cost 50 US dollar. He was really _____ by the price. By mistake, he gave the cashier a 20 US dollar bill instead of a fifty. He was a little _____. Then there was rubbish all over the stadium. The trash was _____.

The people next him made a phone call during the match, which was _____. Joey finally found the football match too _____. He liked staying at home and playing games. They were _____.

E Test yourself

Task 1. Please put the sentences into the right order. The first one has been done for you.

(1) This is the Bell Captain's Desk. May I help you?

(   ) This is Mary speaking. I am going to check out. Could you arrange to have my luggage brought down?

(   ) Yes, it is Room 502.

(   ) My pleasure, Madam.

(   ) No problem. I will reserve one for you right away. After you finish checking out, a taxi will collect you from the hotel and drive you to the airport.

(   ) OK, we'll send a bellboy immediately.

(   ) It's so nice of you.

(   ) Thank you. By the way, could you please order a taxi for me now? I have a plane to catch at 2pm.

(   ) Certainly, Madam. May I have your room number, please?

Task 2. Scan the QR code and interpret what you hear from Chinese into English or from English into Chinese.

扫码听音频

(1) _____
(2) _____
(3) _____
(4) _____
(5) _____
(6) _____

Activity 2   Acquire Serving Skills

A The serving skills—offering concierge services for VIP check-in

Step one: Check the VIP rooms one hour prior to the VIP guests' arrival. Make sure the special arrangement such as flowers, welcome cake, chocolate, etc. as well as the personalized toiletries.

Step two: Pre-register the VIP guests and place the registration card in the room together with the room key or key card.

Step three: Keep close contact with the airport representative to confirm the exact arrival time and car number.

Step four: Remind the housekeeping department to open the room door upon the arrival.

Step five: Have the assistant Manager/ guest relation officer stand by at the main entrance. And greet the guests by their names.

Step six: Escort the guests to the rooms and explain the room facilities to the guests.

Step seven: Help the guests to fill out the registration card, and collect it 10 minutes after the VIP enter the room.

Step eight: Courtesy calls should be made by the assistant manager/guest relation officer.

B The Services a butler can do for VIP guests

1. Offer pre-arrival butler forms for VIP guests to fill out, ensuring that the butler is prepared for any special requests such as dietary restrictions, baby-sitting needs, or special occasions.
2. Anticipate the need of frequent VIP guests and ensure those needs are met even before check-in.
3. Provide a cell phone or an app on the in-room tablet, so that VIP guests can communicate on-the-go or with privacy.
4. Work with all related departments (housekeeping, food services, etc.) to meet VIP guests' needs.

C Special tip

It happens that some guests store their luggage in the hotel for a long time. Below is a long-term luggage storage form. Work with your partner and fill in the form.

Long-Term Luggage Storage Form

Name:	Contact Details:
Article:	Pieces:
Reservation No.:	Room No.:
Storage Date:	Expected Pick Up Date:
Pick Up By:	Contact Details:

Hereby request luggage storage. The sole purpose of this is to enable the guests' luggage to be kept in storage.

Description	Qnty.	Storage Date	Staff	Guest (signature)	Pick up Date	Pick up by (signature)	Staff

The guest understands the terms and conditions that:

1) The maximum duration of storage is two months;

2) The hotel will not be held responsible for any missing or damage items inside the luggage.

Signature: _____

Staff: _____   Date: _____

Activity 3 Practical Training

A Receive the tasks—role play

Task 1. Getting to know your guest

In order to provide better service, the butler decides to ask about the VIP guest's needs and generate service needs. Having learnt that the VIP guest enjoys classic music very much, the butler decides to make some suggestions and preparations.

Task 2. Providing your service

After escorting the VIP guest to his/her room, the butler asks for the guest's permission to unpack his/her luggage and properties. The guest gives his/her consent, and also requests private bartending services.

Useful expressions

- My name is ***, and I am your personal butler.
- Please feel free to let me know if there's anything you need.
- Would you like me to book a concert ticket for you and iron you suit?
- May I unpack your luggage and put it in the wardrobe, please?
- What kind of drinks do you prefer?
- It's my pleasure to be at your service.

B Training card

Name:	Class:	Date:
Your role:	Partner's role:	
Your task:		
Your process:		

(continue)

Conversation between the butler and the VIP guest:

Activity 4 Evaluate Your Study

No.	Tasks	Self-assessment	Group assessment	Teacher evaluation
1	I can tell the main duties of concierges.			
2	I can tell the working procedure of concierges.			
3	I can introduce hotel facilities and services to VIP guests.			
4	I can explain butler service for VIP guests.			
5	I can grasp the words and expressions on concierges.			

Scene 2 Convention and Exhibition

Activity 1 Activate Language Knowledge

A Look at the pictures related to hotel equipments, write down the correct vocabulary as quickly as possible

(1)_____

(2)_____

(3)_____

(4) _____   (5) _____   (6) _____

  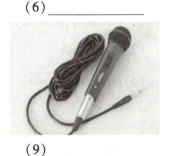

(7) _____   (8) _____   (9) _____

B Scan the QR code and listen to the conversation

Guest: Good morning. Would you please find a room for our business meeting?

Concierge: Certainly, sir. How many people will attend the meeting?

扫码听音频

Guest: Well, about 18.

Concierge: Fine. We have a conference room which can seat up to 20 people.

Guest: That's great. I also need an interpreter.

Concierge: No problem, sir.

Guest: How about the charge of your conference room.

Concierge: It is 100 RMB per hour. There is no minimum charge. Do you want to book it?

Guest: Yes, I think so.

Concierge: May I have your name and room number, please, sir?

Guest: Mr. Black, Room 6868.

Concierge: OK. Please let me show you the facilities in the conference room.

Guest: Thank you. What meeting equipment do you have?

Concierge: Our meeting hall is multifunctional and fully equipped, providing an overhead projector, wireless microphones, projection screens, etc.

Guest: Do you offer audio and video equipment?

Concierge: Yes. Our meeting rooms are all equipped with up-to-date audio and video devices.

Guest: Oh, that's great.

Task 1. Discussion with classmates

1. What do you need to introduce when a guest asks for a conference room?

2. What do you need to introduce when a guest asks about the meeting equipment?

3. What could you do when a guest asks for some meeting equipment that the hotel doesn't have?

Task 2. Practice with teammates

What kinds of meeting equipment can be found in the conference room? Please tick the box(es).

(1) overhead projector ☐

(2) microphone ☐

(3) projection screen ☐

C Read the passage on convention service

Convention services are always related with all-sized meeting room rental, convention equipment rental (such as laptop computers, projectors, screens, white-boards with mark pens, roving microphones, etc.), and sometimes catering service. Meeting rooms are usually equipped with 24 hours Internet access and direct-dial multi-line telephones with voice mail to meet the requirements of efficiency-oriented customers. Translation and interpretation service are also provided by the business center. Some five-star business centers are equipped with the simultaneous interpretation booth in their meeting rooms.

扫码听音频

The procedure of the convention service is as follows:

1. Greet the guest.
2. Ask for more details about the opening ceremony.
3. Agree to arrange a large multi-function hall and a reception room for the opening ceremony
4. Promise to meet the requirements of catering service.
5. Tell the guest the rough rates.
6. Tell the guest when the contract will be sent to him.
7. Say Goodbye.

Note

rental	n.	租赁
catering	n.	饮食服务
simultaneous	n.	同步的
booth	n.	小隔间
multi-functional hall		多功能厅
rough	adj.	大致的
rate	n.	价格

Decide whether the statements are true(T) or false(F) after reading.

( ) 1. Convention services are not related with catering service.
( ) 2. Meeting rooms are usually equipped with 24 hours Internet access.
( ) 3. Translation and interpretation service are not provided by the business center.
( ) 4. The convention service includes telling the guest the rough rates.

D Language tip

当我们要表达"与……相关"时，具体取决于语境和需要强调的内容。以下是一些常见的表达方式及其例子：

1. related to 关联到……
   例句：This study is related to the effects of climate change on marine life.
   这项研究与气候变化对海洋生物的影响有关。
2. involved in/with 涉及到……
   例句：She has been involved with projects related to renewable energy.
   她参与了与可再生能源相关的项目。
4. associated with 与……有关
   例句：The company is associated with several charitable organizations.
   这家公司与几个慈善组织有关。
5. closely linked with/to 与……密切相关
   例句：His research is closely linked with advancements in medical technology.
   他的研究与医疗技术的进展密切相关。

Please fill in the blanks with the given phrases to make complete sentences.

   related to   involved in/with   associated with   closely linked with/to

1. This book is _____ the history of ancient civilizations.
2. She has been _____ projects related to community development.
3. The festival is _____ traditional music and dance performances.
4. Economic growth is closely _____ employment rates.

E Test yourself

Task 1. Put the sentences into the right order. The first one has been done for you

(1) Can I help you?
(   ) Yes, it is.
(   ) Yes, thank you.
(   ) We'd like to book one large conference hall. We need a projector and a video camera.

103

(　　) Yes, we're going to hold a conference.

(　　) What size of conference will you have? We have two large conference halls and three small meeting rooms.

(　　) Next Monday… Is it October 1st?

(　　) I see. What about the time of the conference?

(　　) You're welcome, sir. We look forward to serving you.

(　　) OK, could you sign here?

(　　) Next Monday.

Task 2. Scan the QR code and interpret what you hear from Chinese into English or from English into Chinese

扫码听音频

(1) _____
(2) _____
(3) _____
(4) _____
(5) _____
(6) _____

Activity 2　Acquire Serving Skills

A　The serving skills—preparing meeting

Step one: Learn about the basic situation of the meeting.

　　The organizer of the conference and the name of the conference;

　　The number of people attending the meeting and the time of the conference;

　　The requirements for tea and water at the meeting;

　　The meeting room layout requirements.

Step two: Pay attention to conference room layout.

　　Make the meeting room clean and sanitary;

　　Arrange the conference tables and seating according to the number of meeting guests;

　　Prepare the microphone and debug the amplification equipment;

　　Decorate the conference room with pot plants.

Step three: Prepare and place the supplies.

　　According to the number of people attending the meeting, prepare sufficient tea cups, tea, towels, ashtrays and so on;

　　Conference materials and stationery (paper, notebook, pen) should be arranged in advance according to the requirements of the organizer;

If name cards are needed, it should be made and placed according to the requirements of the organizer.

Step four: Check.

A comprehensive and careful inspection should be carried out.

If errors or omissions are found, they should be corrected immediately.

Finally, the staff should check their appearance and wait for the arrival of the guests.

B Meeting layout

When it comes to planning a meeting, choosing the right seating layout is one of the few matters that need to be addressed from the start.

1. The theatre style is the common setting for conferences, seminars, and annual meetings since it can accommodate a lot of attendees without relying on extensive note-taking.

Pros:

Host a larger audience.

All the seats are facing forwards and towards the center stage.

Maximize the seating capacity of the meeting room.

Cons:

No provision for note taking or consumption of food and beverage.

Aisles are required. Audience interaction is limited.

2. When it comes to training sessions, the U-shaped layout might be of great use.

Pros:

Stimulate high interaction within the group.

Best set up to view audiovisual presentations.

Best suitable for role-playing and physical activities.

Cons:

Hard to set up depending on the shape of the room.

Require more spaces than other layouts.

Only accommodate a few participants.

C Special tip

A meeting agenda is a list of activities that participants are hoping to accomplish during their meeting. Here are some tips for planning an effective agenda for your next team meeting:

1. Make the meeting objectives clear.

2. List agenda topics as questions or tasks.

3. Clarify expectations and responsibilities.

4. Estimate a realistic amount of time for each topic.

5. Get feedback from your team.

Here's an outline that you can tailor to nearly any type of meeting. After reading it, please try to write a meeting agenda by yourself.

MEETING AGENDA
Date: Time: Location:
AGENDA DETAILS
Goals:
1. Agenda item one description

Time:
 Purpose:
 Leader:
    a. Remarks
    b. Remarks
    c. Remarks

2. Agenda item two description

Time:
 Purpose:
 Leader:
    a. Remarks
    b. Remarks
    c. Remarks

3. Agenda item three description

Time:
 Purpose:
 Leader:
    a. Remarks
       i. Additional remarks
       ii. Additional remarks
    b. Remarks
    c. Remarks

4. End of meeting review

Time:
 Purpose:
 Leader:
    a. What did we do well in this meeting?
    b. What should we do differently next meeting?

Module 4   Concierge礼宾

Activity 3   Practical Training

A Receive the tasks—role play

Task 1. The introduction of meeting equipment

A guest plans to hold a meeting with 40 people. He wants to obtain information about the meeting equipment. The clerk of the hotel discusses with the guest about the meeting equipment.

Task 2. The registration for a conference

A guest comes to register for a conference. The clerk checks the guest's information and answers questions about the conference for the guest.

Useful expressions

- We'd like to hold our convention in your hotel.
- What visual and acoustic equipment do you offer?
- It's equipped with overhead projectors, moving microphones and other meeting equipment.
- Let me check, please wait a moment.
- When and where does the conference begin?
- We look forward to serving you.

B Training card

Name:	Class:		Date:
Your role:		Partner's role:	
Your task:			
Your process:			
Conversation between the guest (your partner) and the clerk (you).			

107

Activity 4 Evaluate Your Study

No.	Tasks	Self-assessment	Group assessment	Teacher evaluation
1	I can introduce meeting facilities to guests.			
2	I can tell the conference service procedure.			
3	I can tell the details of meeting preparation and layout.			
4	I can write a meeting agenda.			
5	I can master vocabularies and expressions on conference service.			

Scene 3 Providing Information

Activity 1 Activate Language Knowledge

A Look at the pictures related to hotel facilities, write down the correct vocabulary as quickly as possible

(1)＿＿＿＿＿＿   (2)＿＿＿＿＿＿   (3)＿＿＿＿＿＿

(4)＿＿＿＿＿＿   (5)＿＿＿＿＿＿

Module 4 Concierge礼宾

B Scan the QR code and listen to the conversation

Guest: Can you give me some sightseeing advice?

Concierge: It's my pleasure, Madam. Is this your first time to Guangzhou?

Guest: Yes. Is there any place of interest nearby?

Concierge: Let me see... There is a Mausoleum of Southern China Emperor nearby, with a history of over 2,300 years.

Guest: This sounds great! If the weather is fine, I'll visit it tomorrow.

Concierge: Hope you enjoy your visit!

Guest: By the way. Where can I have salon services?

Concierge: We have a Beauty Salon on the 6th floor. You can go straight out of the elevator and it is on your right.

Guest: Thank you. What kinds of service do you have there?

Concierge: The Salon offers a variety of hair and nail services, including styling, haircuts, manicures and pedicures.

Guest: It sounds wonderful. Oh, I am leaving Guangzhou next Monday. 15th May. Will you please book a ticket to Paris for me?

Concierge: Yes, madam. Let me see. There are several flights to Paris available on 15th May. Which fight do you prefer?

Guest: Afternoon flights preferably.

Concierge: Yes, madam. There are two flights available that day. One is at 4 pm, and the other one is at 9 pm.

Guest: Well, I'd like the 4 pm one.

Concierge: No problem. I'll fix your ticket, madam. Please wait a moment.

Guest: OK. Thank you.

Task 1. Discussion with classmates

1. What are the must-have qualities of a concierge when providing information for guests?

2. What do you do when a guest is unsatisfied with your sightseeing advice?

3. What do you do when a guest makes an unusual request, such as searching for hard-to-find items?

Task 2. Practice with teammates

1. What kinds of information should a concierge provide? Please tick the box(es).

(1) local events and activities ☐   (2) medical advice ☐

(3) means of transportation ☐ (4) money-saving tips ☐
(5) hotel facilities and services ☐

C Read the passage on providing information as a concierge

A hotel concierge handles many aspects of guests' stay at a hotel. One such aspect is providing information and making suggestions.

A concierge should provide guests with suggestions for recreation and various services within the hotel itself and in the surrounding geographical area. Therefore, it is very important that a concierge know the local restaurants, interesting attractions, and other sorts of services available in the region.

Excellent communication skills are also critical for a concierge when giving advice. It is important to speak clearly, and maintain a positive tone and a helpful attitude. Being a good communicator also means being a good listener. In other words, concierges need to listen carefully to their guests' needs and requests. Only in this way can they be able to proactively identify any particular support they may require, offer valuable suggestions and provide a positive experience for guests.

Note

recreation	n. 娱乐；消遣
geographical	adj. 地理的
maintain	v. 维持，保持
tone	n. 语气，腔调
proactively	adv. 主动地，前摄地

Decide whether the statements are true(T) or false(F) after reading.

(　) 1. Concierges need to meet a variety of guests' requirements.
(　) 2. Concierges should be an expert in geography.
(　) 3. When a guest is making requests, a concierge should listen carefully and identify their needs.
(　) 4. It is important for concierges to give advice in a clear and understandable way.

D Language tip

1. handles，表示处理，应付(局势、人、工作或感情)。
　　例句：To tell the truth, I don't know if I can handle the job.

2. provide somebody with something. 表示向某人供给或供应某物。

例句：Books provide children with ideas and a stimulus for play.

3. It is important that.... 表示……是重要的。

例句：It is important that he should attend every day.

4. be critical for. 表示对……至关重要。

例句：The next two weeks will be critical for the hotel.

5. In other words. 表示换句话说。

例句：They asked him to leave — in other words he was fired.

Choose the correct verbs for the following sentences.

1. She didn't **hand/handle** the situation quite well.

2. It's the concierge's job to **provide** the customers **to/with** the information they need.

3. It is important **that/on** you help with the cleaning.

4. It is critical **for/of** the manager to give David another chance.

5. **In/On** other words, this is the most beautiful wedding I have ever been to.

E Test yourself

Task 1. Put the sentences into the right order. The first one has been done for you.

(1) Good morning. This is the Concierge speaking. How can I help you?

(   ) Then you can go to visit the West Lake. It's famous for its natural scenery.

(   ) It's my pleasure. Hope you have a nice trip.

(   ) Sure. How many days will you stay here?

(   ) Thank you so much.

(   ) Of course. I'll call you back in a few minutes.

(   ) Three days I suppose.

(   ) This is Room 8013. Can you give me some advice on tourist attractions? I am new to this city.

(   ) Sounds like a good idea. Could you contact the travel agency for me and tell me the expense?

Task 2. Scan the QR code and interpret what you hear from Chinese into English or from English into Chinese.

(1) _____

(2) _____

(3) _____

(4) _____

(5) _____

(6) _____

Activity 2 Acquire Serving Skills

A Booking flight tickets for guests

It is the Concierge team's responsibility to know the correct standard for handling a guest's request for flight ticket booking.

1. Complete visitor introduction form, including the following information:

Destination.

Departure date/time.

The number of passengers.

One way or return ticket included.

Seat class (economy, business class, first class, etc.)

The frequent flyer number of the guest in case applicable.

Any airline preference (if there is more than one airline operating that route).

Any seat preference (non-smoking, aisle, window, and etc.)

Guest registered email ID or mobile number.

2. Send introductory email to travel consultant attaching the visitor introduction form.

3. Book airfare with travel consultant.

4. Pay for airfare.

5. Save and print itinerary, e-ticket, invoice and forward to the guest/visitor.

B Arranging tours for guests

After offering sightseeing advice, some guests may further ask for tour arrangement. Below are the steps of arranging a tour for a guest.

1. Upon receive the guest's request for booking a tour.

2. Information should be listed when taking a tour arrangement.

3. Inform the guest about the tour outcome.

4. Record the tour arrangement.

Inform the guest that the tour has been arranged by phone or leave a message, and remind the guest the start time and the meeting point should be at concierge.

C Special tip

When a guest asks the concierge for sightseeing advice, he/she may also want to rent a car from the hotel for transportation. Below is a hotel car rental form. Work with your partner and fill in the form.

Hotel Car Rental Form

Borrow Date: _____   Borrower: _____
Driving License Number: _____   Expiry Date of License: _____
Car Model: _____   License Plate Number: _____
Return Date: _____   Total Fees: _____

A deposit of _____ RMB will be held by the hotel, either by cash or credit card authorization, upon the guest's rent of the vehicle from the hotel, which would only be refunded upon return of the vehicle in one GOOD working condition.

I understand that the hotel shall assume NO responsibility or liability, in whole or in part, for any possible damage caused.

Guest Signature: _____   *Date*: _____
Front Office Signature: _____   *Date*: _____

Activity 3 Practical Training

A Receive the tasks—role play

Task 1. Booking concert tickets for guests

You are a concierge working in the hotel. A guest is calling the concierge counter to ask for help with booking tickets. The guest wants to go to a concert this evening with his family, but he finds that all the tickets are unavailable on the Internet.

Task 2. Recommending recreational activities

You are a concierge working in the hotel. A guest is calling the concierge counter to ask for advice on recreation. The guest is a high school graduate, who is on a graduation trip with her best friends. She wants the concierge to recommend some affordable and memorable recreational activities.

Useful expressions

- I'll try my best and find a solution for you.
- How many tickets would you like to buy?
- How about going to the concert tomorrow night?

- I am very pleased to suggest that you visit the aquarium and see different kinds of sea life.
- You could try a music festival with your friends.
- Shall I draw a road map for you?
- Hope you enjoy a happy and safe trip.

B Training card

Name:	Class:	Date:
Your role:	Partner's role:	
Your task:		
Your process:		

Conversation between the concierge and the guest.

Activity 4   Evaluate Your Study

No.	Tasks	Self-assessment	Group assessment	Teacher evaluation
1	I can give directions to guests.			
2	I can give sightseeing advice to guests.			
3	I can book tickets for guests.			

No.	Tasks	Self-assessment	Group assessment	Teacher evaluation
				(continue)
4	I can ask about guests' preferences and needs.			
5	I can master vocabularies and expressions on giving sightseeing advice and booking tickets.			

Scene 4　　Finance

Activity 1　Activate Language Knowledge

A Look at the pictures related to the currency names, write down the correct vocabulary as quickly as possible

(1)＿＿＿＿＿＿

(2)＿＿＿＿＿＿

(3)＿＿＿＿＿＿

(4)＿＿＿＿＿＿

(5)＿＿＿＿＿＿

(6)＿＿＿＿＿＿

(7)＿＿＿＿＿＿

(8)＿＿＿＿＿＿

(9)＿＿＿＿＿＿

B Scan the QR code and listen to the conversation

Guest：I'd like to exchange some money.

扫码听音频

Concierge: How much do you want to change?

Guest: 500 US dollars.

Concierge: I'm afraid we don't have that much cash on hand. Could you change a little less today, then come back tomorrow to change the rest?

Guest: OK. What's the most I can change today?

Concierge: Would 100 US dollars be enough?

Guest: Well, I suppose it will have to do. What's the rate today on American dollar?

Concierge: Just a moment, please. I'll check. Today's exchange rate is 7.97 RMB for 1 US dollar.

Guest: Then I want to change 100 US dollars.

Concierge: Certainly. What denominations do you need?

Guest: I need some cens.

Concierge: How about if I give you a fifty and five tens. Will that be enough?

Guest: Yes, that's good. Thank you.

Concierge: Could you sign here, please, and fill in your room number.

(*after a while*)

Concierge: Thank you. Just a moment, please. Here you are. Please count it. And here's your exchange slip.

Task 1. Discussion with classmates

1. What do you need to check when a guest ask for currency exchange?
2. What could you do when the exchange amount is too large?
3. What do you remind the guests to do after currency exchange?

Task 2. Practice with teammates

What kinds of people can have currency exchange at the hotel? Please tick the box.

1. Hotel guest ☐   2. Visitors ☐   3. Hotel staff ☐

C Read the passage on currency exchange

According to China's current administrative regulations, the circulation of foreign currencies is prohibited within the territory of the People's Republic of China, and foreign currency pricing and settlement are not allowed.

In order to facilitate tourists to China and compatriots

扫码听音频

Note

administrative regulations
　　　　　　　　行政法规
circulation　　*n.* 流通
prohibit　　　*v.* 禁止

from Hong Kong, Macao and Taiwan, China and other designated countries not only accept foreign currency, traveler's checks and foreign credit cards for RMB, but also accept the exchange of sterling, Hong Kong dollar, US dollar, euro, Singapore dollar, Japanese yen, Canadian dollar, Australian dollar and other currencies.

Why do hotels provide foreign currency exchange services?

1. Match its facade, star rating, and identity.

2. It is related to the positioning of the hotel and the source market.

3. Through the exchange of this business, the large amount of change needed in the actual operation can be exchanged back as needed.

Therefore, Some hotels in China will provide currency exchange services to meet the need of both the tourists and the hotels.

territory	n.	领土
settlement	n.	（关于钱财转让的）协议（书）
facilitate	v.	促进；使便利
compatriot	n.	同胞
designated	adj.	指定的
exchange	n.	兑换；汇兑
sterling	n.	英镑
facade	n.	表面，外表

Decide whether the statements are true(T) or false(F) after reading.

(   ) 1. Any hotel can provide currency exchange services.

(   ) 2. A customer can change whichever currency he/she wants.

(   ) 3. Currency exchange services is related to the positioning of the hotel.

(   ) 4. In order to facilitate tourists to China and compatriots from Hong Kong, Macao and Taiwan, China and other designated countries, some hotels in China will provide currency exchange services.

D Language tip

Except 和 Beside 的区别：

Except，作介词时，表示"排除"关系，意为除了……之外不再有。

例句：She goes to work every day except Monday. 她除了礼拜一每天都工作。

Beside，作介词时，表示"累加"的除外关系，意为除……外还有。

例句：He has lots of interests besides sports. 他除了体育还有其他很多爱好。

Try to translate the sentences by using the correct word.

1. 她除了狗没有别的宠物。

2. 除了一个鸡蛋，她一天什么都没吃。

_____

3. 我不太想去，况且现在太晚了。

_____

4. 除了旧的 CD，我还找到好多旧书。

_____

E Test yourself

Task 1. Put the sentences into the right order. The first one has been done for you.

(1) Good morning, Madam.

(   ) Just a moment, please. I'll check. Today's exchange rate is 7.12 RMB for 1 US dollar.

(   ) Good morning. I'd like to exchange some money.

(   ) How much do you want to change?

(   ) Thank you and goodbye.

(   ) Here you are. That's 50 US dollars. Please count it. And here's your exchange slip.

(   ) What's the rate today on US dollar?

(   ) Then I want to change 50 US dollars.

(   ) Goodbye and have a nice day.

Task 2. Scan the QR code and interpret what you hear from Chinese into English or from English into Chinese.

扫码听音频

(1) _____
(2) _____
(3) _____
(4) _____
(5) _____
(6) _____

Activity 2   Acquire Serving Skills

A Hotel front desk foreign currency exchange service standard

1. Confirm whether the foreign currency of the guests is the foreign currency accepted by the hotel.

2. Report the foreign exchange rate of the day to the guest.

3. Ask the amount of foreign currency the guest want to exchange.

4. Collect foreign currency cash from the guest.

5. Strictly implement the "multiple counting system" and votes.

6. Calculate the RMB amount that should be exchanged to the guest with the foreign currency cash amount and the foreign currency exchange rate.

7. Ask the guest to show their passports. Check whether the changer is a passport holder.

8. If the guest cash a traveler's check, ask the guests to sign the travelers' check in front of the cashier. The exchange rate of cheques is higher than that of banknotes, and there is a handling charge.

9. Fill in the "foreign currency exchange memo" in quadruplicate (based on the selected bank).

10. Ask the guest to sign the "foreign currency exchange memo", and the cashier should indicate the room number.

B Special tip

You will have to fill in the cash flow statement after finishing the currency change. Please try to fill in the cash flow statement by yourself.

Hotel Exchange Certificate and Exchange Memo

Nationality	Passport No.	Date	Name & Signature	Address/Hotel
Amount in foreign currency	Less discount	Net amount	Rate	Amount in RMB
Particulars				

Please keep this for checking. Part of unused RMB can be reconverted into foreign currency for only once when holder leaves China within six months.

Auditor: Clerk:

🏃 Activity 3 Practical Training

A Receive the tasks—role play

Task 1. Currency exchange service

Mrs Blake is arriving at Grand Hotel and she wants to change 200 US dollars into RMB. The concierge checks the rate and makes the change for her.

Task 2. Turn-down service

Miss Yoko has been living in the hotel for 5 days. Now she is running out of cash. She wants to change 300,000 Yen into RMB. The concierge explains that there isn't enough cash in the hotel and suggests her go to the bank.

酒店英语

Useful expressions

- May I help you, madam?
- The rate today is…
- What's your room number, madam?
- I'm afraid we don't have that much.
- There is a bank… You may try and change currency there.
- How about going to Bank of China around the corner?

B Training card

Name:	Class:	Date:
Your role:	Partner's role:	
Your task:		
Your process:		

Conversation between the guest (your partner) and the concierge (you).

120

Activity 4　Evaluate Your Study

No.	Tasks	Self-assessment	Group assessment	Teacher evaluation
1	I can check the rate and make a currency change for customer.			
2	I know the currency change procedure.			
3	I can fill out the Cash Flow Statement.			
4	I know how to turn down service when the amount is too big.			
5	I can master vocabularies and expressions on currency exchange service.			

Chinese Story

Chinese Etiquette

Every country has a set of rules about etiquette for its own unique culture. As a country that evolved over thousands of years of history, China is no exception. There are mainly three kinds of etiquette in China.

The first category is daily life etiquette. This includes meeting, conversation, dining, gift-giving, and the like. For example, according to the seating etiquette, people in the highest class are placed in the most honorable seats, while those in the lowest class sit further away.

The second category is the festival customs and festival celebration etiquette, such as on Spring Festival, or in one's funeral. Celebration etiquette, particularly during festivals and celebrations are important. When people worship or express their gratitude, they should not only be respectful, reciting congratulations while bending, but also offer a congratulatory gift.

The third category is business etiquette, which covers conference etiquette, negotiation etiquette, guest welcoming and seeing-off etiquette, and knowledge of negotiation taboos, etc. For instance, it is advisable to dress conservative suits and be punctual in business meetings.

A. Based on the pictures given, write down the specific aspects of China etiquette.

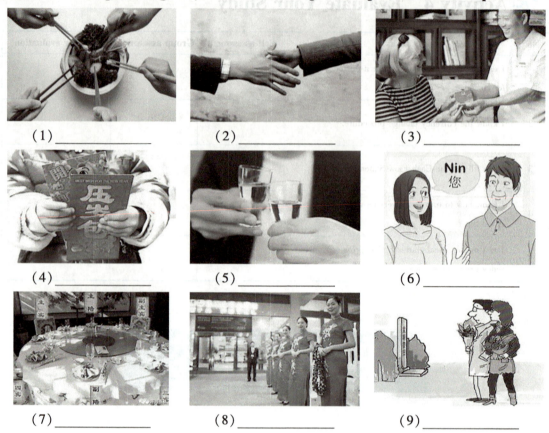

(1) _____ (2) _____ (3) _____

(4) _____ (5) _____ (6) _____

(7) _____ (8) _____ (9) _____

B. Work in pairs and describe the Do and Don't for each etiquette in China.

Etiquette	Do	Don't
Greeting etiquette		
Dining etiquette		
Gift-giving etiquette		
Etiquette on Spring Festival		
Guest-welcoming etiquette		

C. Work in Team.

As front office staff, you and your partners are preparing for a silk exhibition that is to be held in the hotel. Discuss with each other three "golden rules" for hotel etiquette and explain the reasons.

Choose a representative from each group to report "golden rules", and the key steps of preparing silk exhibition.

Module 5

Other Hotel Service
其他酒店服务

? Questions for thinking

1. What is the duty of the customer service department?
2. Do you know the any other hotel service?

Goals

After studying this project, you should be able to:

∨ Write emails and leave messages to guests;
∨ Tell the main duties of a recreation service department;
∨ Describe basic steps for dealing with complaint;
∨ Know how to order things for guests;
∨ Know the business communication etiquette.

Prepare for learning

Scan the following QR code tolearn the new words and take a test on.

扫码听音频

酒店英语

Scene 1   Recreation Service

Activity 1   Activate Language Knowledge

A Look at the pictures of different items in health club & SPA store, write down the correct vocabulary as quickly as possible

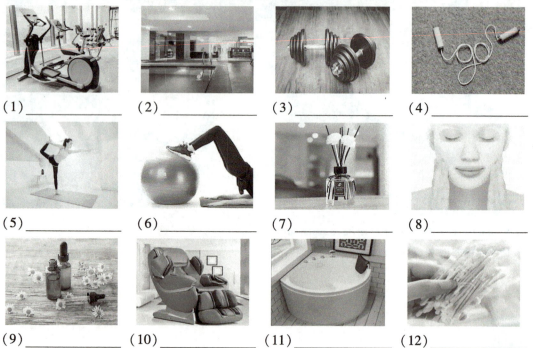

(1) _____   (2) _____   (3) _____   (4) _____

(5) _____   (6) _____   (7) _____   (8) _____

(9) _____   (10) _____   (11) _____   (12) _____

B Scan the QR code and listen to the conversation

扫码听音频

Receptionist: Hello, how can I help you?

Guest: I would like to do some running in the health club.

Receptionist: May I have your room number please?

Guest: Yes, Room 1301. Here is my room card.

Receptionist: Sure, Room 1301. Would you like to take a shower after the running?

Guest: I think so.

Receptionist: Sorry to keep you waiting. Here is the key of your locker, and the towel. Just go straight and you would find the treadmill. To your left is the shower room. Please pay attention to the gentle reminder of locker and fitness equipment.

Guest: I see. Thank you.

126

Receptionist: It's my pleasure. We're always at your service.

Task 1. Discussion with classmates

1. Where is the treadmill?
2. What is the guest's room number?
3. What does the receptionist give the guest?

Task 2. Practice with teammates

Write down the sequence of checking in the health club service.

(1) take the key of locker　　　　(2) show the room card

(3) read the gentle reminder　　　(4) express your intention

_____

C　Read the passage on fitness center

A good fitness center is a place where guests can work on self-improvement. They may want to lose weight, gain muscle, or enjoy the self-confidence that comes from working out.

Hotels can achieve this idea of self-improvement by building their health club. A hotel brand fitness club will draw more guests into the fitness area than a gym that looks thrown together. It also provides hotels with an opportunity to add offerings such as specialized workout equipment or Wi-Fi-enabled machinery.

Daily or bi-weekly fitness classes are an easy way to engage with guests through a fun activity. Yoga, Pilates, and even dance workouts can all be done inside an open gym space that can double as a multi-purpose room when the classes aren't in session.

Local fitness classes that take place in hotels make that hotel stand out from the competition. They also result in returning guests, who will prefer to stay where they can continue taking the classes they do at home.

Note

self-improvement	n. 自我完善
muscle	n. 肌肉
work out	n. 锻炼
specialized	adj. 专业的
machinery	n. 机械
engage with	与……接洽
Pilates	n. 普拉提
multi-purpose	adj. 多用途的；多功能的
stand out	脱颖而出
result in	导致

Decide whether the statements are true (T) or false (F) after reading.

( ) 1. A good fitness center is not a place where guests can work on self-improvement.
( ) 2. Daily or bi-weekly fitness classes are an easy way to engage with guests through an interesting activity.
( ) 3. Guests may enjoy the self-confidence that comes from working out.
( ) 4. Yoga, Pilates, and even dance workouts can be done outside an open gym space.

D Language tip

有时我们在提供酒店服务时不得不打断(别人)。因此，学会(如何)礼貌地打断别人是至关重要的。以下列出了一些常见结构：

I'm so sorry to interrupt but…
I don't mean to be rude but may I interrupt quickly?
Sorry to interrupt but may I ask a quick question?
Excuse me but may I jump in here?
I'm so sorry for interrupting but I'd like to make sure I understood you correctly.

Choose the correct forms to complete the sentences.

1. I don't mean to **be/being** rude but may I interrupt quickly?
2. I'm so sorry for **interrupting/interrupt**.
3. I'm **terribly/terrible** sorry to interrupt you.
4. Sorry to interrupt but **may/do** I ask a quick question?
5. Excuse me but may I jump **in/on** here?

E Test yourself

Task 1. Put the sentences into the right order. The first one has been done for you.

(1) Good afternoon. How can I help you?
( ) It's Room 1303.
( ) Good afternoon. Can I book the SPA service tonight?
( ) Sure. What is your room number?
( ) OK, Room 1303. Would you like to have some SPA service in the club?
( ) Of course, sir. You have booked the health club & massage service.
( ) Yes, please. I would like to have a massage.
( ) Goodbye.
( ) Thank you and goodbye.
( ) Yes, that is right.

Module 5 Other Hotel Service其他酒店服务

Task 2. Scan the QR code and interpret what you hear from Chinese into English or from English into Chinese.

(1) _____
(2) _____
(3) _____
(4) _____
(5) _____
(6) _____

Activity 2 Acquire Serving Skills

A The serving skills—booking health club service procedure

Step one: Pick up the phone.
Step two: Greet the guest.
Step three: Ask the guest about health condition.
Step four: Ask the guest whether to book for gym, swimming pool or training class.
Step five: Tell the guest about the available hours.
Step six: Take down all the info you get from the guest.
Step seven: Tell the guest that the booking is successful.
Step eight: Say goodbye to the guest.

B Tips for keeping guests' safe

Here are some tips to create a balance between keeping visitors having fun and keeping them safe.

1. **Training staff**: The first step to securing safety is to train the employees on how they can recognise and eliminate risks around the building.

2. **Educating guests**: To educate guests on potential risks and how to avoid them. Ensure that they understand their safety and security responsibilities.

3. **First Aid**: Because injuries can happen at any time, it's important to make first aid accessible to everyone on the property. Remember to place first aid boxes close to areas with high risks of injuries including the gym and swimming pool.

C Special tip

　　This form is a sample agreement for membership to a health and/or fitness facility,
Sample:

129

APPLICANT

First Name: _____ Last Name: _____
Residence: _____
City: _____ Province: _____ Zipcode: _____
Home Telephone: _____ Business Telephone: _____
Email Address: _____
Credit Card Number: _____
Expiration Date: _____
Club mail should be sent to: _____

TYPE OF MEMBERSHIP

☐ Individual ☐ Couples ☐ 1 Year Prepaid

Start Date: _____
Initiation Fee: _____
Monthly Dues: _____
Prorated Dues Paid: _____
Total Amount Paid: _____

Activity 3 Practical Training

A Receive the tasks—role play

Task 1. Booking Health Club service

The receptionist is going to turn down the request from Mr. White. Mr. White would like to change the time of service he books. He asks the receptionist to change his booking from 9 am to 11 am for he cannot make it that early. The receptionist tells him 11 am to 12 am is fully booked and he can only change the booking to 3 pm.

Task 2. Booking SPA service

The guest greets the receptionist and ask the receptionist whether the hotel has the SPA and massage service. The receptionist tells that massage service charges additional fees and can book the service any time from the afternoon till 10 pm. And the guest can use the coupon on the TV desk in the guest's room.

Useful expressions

- Just a moment, please. I'll check the availability for you.
- I'm afraid we're fully booked for that time.
- Is it possible for you to change the time?
- Let me check if we have any vacancy.
- Would you like to make a reservation at another time?
- We hope we'll have another opportunity to serve you.

B Training card

Name:	Class:	Date:
Your role:	Partner's role:	

Your task:

Your process:

Conversation between the guest (your partner) and the receptionist (you).

Activity 4 Evaluate Your Study

No.	Tasks	Self-assessment	Group assessment	Teacher evaluation
1	I can tell the main duties of a receptionist on health club and SPA service.			
2	I can tell the health club & SPA booking procedure.			
3	I can understand what is Green Hotel.			
4	I can tell the details of booking SPA & health club.			
5	I can master vocabularies and expressions on health club & SPA service.			

Scene 2   Handling Complaints

Activity 1   Activate Language Knowledge

A Look at the pictures of different items in handling complaints, write down the correct phrases as quickly as possible

(1)_____   (2)_____   (3)_____

(4)_____   (5)_____   (6)_____

Module 5 Other Hotel Service 其他酒店服务

B Scan the QR code and listen to the conversation

Guest：Good morning, sir.

Receptionist：How may I help you?

Guest：Yes, I just checked in and this room is unacceptable. It's Room 1666.

Receptionist：Is there anything wrong with the room?

Guest：Yes, there certainly is. We requested a non-smoking room, but the room smells really bad.

Receptionist：Let me check. Yes, Room 1666 is supposed to be a non-smoking room.

Guest：Well, somebody surely didn't follow the rules. The curtain smells like cigars. We can hardly breath and the windows can't open at all.

Receptionist：I am really sorry about that. I will change another room for you.

Guest：Yes, please.

Receptionist：OK, I will update your room to the presidential suite as a compensation. Here is the room card.

Guest：Thank you very much.

Receptionist：You are welcome. I am really sorry for the inconvenience it has caused you.

Task 1. Discussion with classmates

1. What is the complaint about?

2. What is the guest's room number?

3. How does the receptionist deal with the complaint?

Task 2. Practice with teammates

Write down the sequence of dealing with the complaints.

（1）explain the fault　　　　　　（2）propose to settle the problem

（3）acknowledge the problem　　　（4）apologize for the error or fault

C Read the passage on hotel customer complaints

What is hotel complaint? hotel customer complaints are often a sign that there's a disconnection between what customers expected and what hotel delivered. Complaints about a hotel can and should be made to management when your experience is not up to normal standards.

Note

deliver　v. 发表；递送

If you have an unpleasant hotel stay, you can directly complaint to hotel employees, like the front desk worker or manager. You can also complain to higher managers if the hotel is a franchised company.

While you may not be able to have the problem fixed during your stay, the hotel may offer you a consolation for your troubles, such as a meal voucher or a few complimentary nights.

By dealing with hotel staff appropriately, by escalating your complaint, and by sharing your unhappiness with the broader community, you'll be able to make sure your complaint is heard and the problem is well on its way to being fixed.

unpleasant	adj.	不愉快的
franchise	v.	授予（或出售）特许经销权（或经营权）
fix	v.	修理
consolation	n.	安慰；慰藉
voucher	n.	代金券
complimentary	adj.	免费的；赠送的
escalate	v.	逐步升级；（使）逐步扩大

Decide whether the statements are true(T) or false(F) after reading.

(　　) 1. If you have an unpleasant hotel stay, you can direct complaints to hotel employees.

(　　) 2. While you may not be able to have the problem addressed during your stay, the hotel may offer you a consolation for your troubles, such as a meal voucher.

(　　) 3. Customer complaints are often a sign that there's a connection between what customers expected and what you delivered.

(　　) 4. By dealing with hotel staff appropriately, customers' complaint can not be fixed.

D Language tip

表示道歉的几种方式：

1. **Sorry / I'm sorry**: the usual way of apologizing to someone you know well.
2. **I do apologize for…**: a more polite and formal way of apologizing, used especially when you feel responsible for something that someone else has done.
3. **Excuse me**: used when apologizing for something you did accidentally.
4. **I beg your pardon**: a more formal way of apologizing for something you did accidentally.
5. **I/We owe you an apology**: used when you realize you have treated someone badly, for example by blaming them for something that is not their fault.
6. **Please accept my/our apologies**: used when making a written or formal apology.
7. **I/We regret…**: used when making an apology in an official announcement.

Choose the correct form to complete sentences.

1. I do apologize **for/to** Jack's behaviour.

Module 5 Other Hotel Service 其他酒店服务

2. I beg your pardon, I didn't mean **to/for** interrupt.

3. We've found who the thief was, and it seems we **owe/own** you an apology.

4. We accept that this is the company's fault and ask you to **accept/give** our sincere apologies.

5. We regret to **announcing/ announce** that tonight's performance has been cancelled.

E Test yourself

Task 1. Put the sentences into the right order. The first one has been done for you.

(1) Good afternoon, sir. What can I do for you?

(　) You are welcome. I am really sorry for the inconvenience it has caused you.

(　) Yes, please. Thank you very much.

(　) Yes, there certainly is. We requested a non-smoking room, but the room smells badly.

(　) Well, somebody surely didn't follow the rules. The curtain has a disgusting smell. We can hardly breath and the windows can't open at all.

(　) I am really sorry about that. I will change another room for you.

(　) Is there anything wrong with the room?

(　) Let me check. Yes, Room 1668 is supposed to be a non-smoking room.

(　) Yes, I just checked in and this room is unacceptable. It's Room 1668.

Task 2. Scan the QR code and interpret what you hear from Chinese into English or from English into Chinese.

扫码听音频

(1) _____

(2) _____

(3) _____

(4) _____

(5) _____

(6) _____

Activity 2　Acquire Serving Skills

A The serving skills—dealing with complaints

Step one：Greet the customers and try your best to remain as calm as possible to help.

Step two：Ask what happened.

Step three：Listen to the guest patiently and take down problems in detail sincerely and seriously.

Step four：Express your regret and apology, find the real source of the complaint.

Step five：Make a plan with the customer to follow up his/her complaint.

Step six：Express your regret again. Offer solutions without delay.

Step seven: Follow up to confirm that the problem was resolved.

B The details when dealing with complaints

1. Listen and take notes. Write down any names, dates, and major points of the complaints.
2. Express your regret for the guests' dissatisfaction and any convenience he or she may have experienced.
3. Think twice before making promises.
4. Check the facts.
5. Offer solutions. There are many different types of solutions which could turn a disappointed customer into a happy one, such as, to offer a replacement, refund the money, offer a repair, offer a discount on the next purchase, and apologize for the inconvenience caused.

C Special tip

Reply to letters of complaint, often called "letter of adjustment", must be handled carefully. The sample of letter of adjustment is as follow:

Sample:

> Dear Mr. Black,
> Thank you for _____ of July 12.
> We are _____ the room you booked smell badly.
> As a result of our investigation, some housemaid might secretly smoke in that room before.
> We would like to _____ a presidential suite as soon as possible.
> Please accept our _____ for the inconvenience it has caused.
>
> Yours sincerely,
> Demi
> Customer Service Manager

Activity 3   Practical Training

A Receive the tasks—role play

Task 1. Complaint about smell

You are a customer service representative. Mr Black comes to complain that there is a bad smell of the sheet and it seems like someone just smoked in this non-smoking room. You need to apologize and upgrade the room for him.

Task 2. Complaint about housemaid service

You are a customer service representative. **Mr Black complaints that housemaid** did not knock the door and ask him whether the room can be cleaned now. She just unlocked the door and began cleaning. The guest doesn't want to clean the room now. You need to apologize and promise to give the coupon as a compensation.

Useful expressions

- We must sincerely apologize for...
- Please accept our apologies for...
- I am really sorry for the inconvenience it has caused you...
- As a result of investigation, we found that...
- The cause of/reason for the mistake was...
- To show goodwill, we would like to... /we are willing to... we are prepared to...

B Training card

Name:	Class:	Date:
Your role:	Partner's role:	
Your task:		
Your process:		

(continue)

Conversation between the guest (your partner) and the housemaid (you).

Activity 4 Evaluate Your Study

No.	Tasks	Self-assessment	Group assessment	Teacher evaluation
1	I can tell the main duties of a receptionist on customer complaint service.			
2	I can tell the procedure of dealing with customer complaints.			
3	I can tell what is TQM.			
4	I can tell the details of dealing with complaints.			
5	I can master vocabularies and expressions on customer complaints.			

Scene 3 Sales and Marketing

Activity 1 Activate Language Knowledge

A Look at the pictures of different situations in communicating and marketing, write down the correct vocabulary or phrases as quickly as possible

(1) _____   (2) _____   (3) _____

Module 5 Other Hotel Service 其他酒店服务

(4)＿＿＿＿＿＿

(5)＿＿＿＿＿＿

B Scan the QR code and listen to the conversation

扫码听音频

Receptionist: Hello, this is Four Season Hotel.

Sara: Hello. I'd like to make an appointment to visit Mr. Black, the customer service manager, please.

Receptionist: Have you been here before?

Sara: No, I haven't.

Receptionist: OK. Can I have your name please?

Sara: It's Sara Wang.

Receptionist: Mr. Black won't have any openings until 3:30 pm this afternoon. Is that OK?

Sara: I am sorry that I can't make it this afternoon. How about tomorrow?

Receptionist: A minute, please. Mr. Black is available at 10:30 am tomorrow morning.

Sara: Yes, that would be fine.

Receptionist: OK. We'll see you at 10:30 am tomorrow.

Sara: Thank you. Goodbye.

Task 1. Discussion with classmates

1. What would Sara like to do?
2. Is Sara free this afternoon?
3. What is the final appointment time?

Task 2. Practice with teammates

Write down the sequence of making an appointment.

(1) set a day and time for the appointment

(2) give thanks

(3) agree to the day and time

(4) state who you are and the wish to make an appointment

C Read the passage on customer visits

Two Potential Goals of Your Hotel Customer Visit

Going into a customer visit with goals in mind will help you get the most out of your time there. Here are two goals to consider when planning a customer visit:

1. Understanding Their Business Goals

If you're visiting a client, you're likely hoping for a long term relationship. Understanding what their future goals are can help align your service with their needs. These in-depth conversations would rarely come up over a quick phone call.

2. Gathering Feedback

Customer visits provide a unique opportunity to gather honest and in-the-moment insight into what your customers need and want. When you sit next to customer, there's a lot more space to have this feedback arise. And documenting it for future sales opportunities and your product team is one of the more productive actions you can take during a customer visit.

Note

potential goal 潜在的目标

long term 长期

align　　v. 排列；校准；
　　　　　　排整齐

in-depth　adj. 彻底的；
　　　　　　深入详尽的

unique　adj. 唯一的；独一无
　　　　　　二的；独特的；
　　　　　　罕见的

insight　n. 洞察力；领悟；
　　　　　　洞悉；了解

Decide whether the statements are true(T) or false(F) after reading.

(　　) 1. If you're visiting a client, you're not likely hoping for a long term relationship.

(　　) 2. Understanding what their future goals are can help align your product with their needs.

(　　) 3. Customer visits provide a unique opportunity to gather honest and in-the-moment insight into what your customers need and want.

(　　) 4. Documenting the feedback for future sales opportunities and your product team is not one of the more productive actions.

D Language tip

不定式 to do 的三种用法：

1. 在形容词后加上不定式"to do"，即：形容词 + 不定式"to do"。

　　例句：It's **fun to spend** time with friends.

2. 用不定式"to do"表示做某事的目的或理由。

　　例句：I **went** to the shops **to buy** some milk.

3. 在量词后使用不定式"to do"，结构是：量词 + 名词 + 不定式"to do"。

　　例句：I have too **many emails to send.**

Module 5 Other Hotel Service 其他酒店服务

To finish the sentences with the given words.

1. There are few pencils left in the studio _____ (draw) blueprints with.
2. It't helpful _____ (eat) garlic soup.
3. Don't make that face _____ (scare) him!
4. There isn't enough time _____ (get) to the station.
5. I am working _____ (save) money.
6. It' necessary _____ (see) a dentist if you have a toothache.

E Test yourself

Task 1. put the sentences into the right order. The first one has been done for you.

(1) Hello, this is Black Swan Hotel.
(   ) OK. Can I have your name please?
(   ) Hello. I'd like to make an appointment to visit Mr. Black, the customer service manager, please.
(   ) Mr. Black has opening at 4:30 pm this afternoon. Is that ok?
(   ) Have you been here before?
(   ) Thank you. Goodbye.
(   ) Yes, that would be fine.
(   ) It's Sally Chou.
(   ) I am sorry that I can't make it this afternoon. How about tomorrow?
(   ) OK. We'll see you at 11:30 am tomorrow morning.
(   ) A minute, please. Mr. Black is available at 11:30 am tomorrow morning.

Task 2. Scan the QR code and interpret what you hear from Chinese into English or from English into Chinese.

扫码听音频

(1) _____
(2) _____
(3) _____
(4) _____
(5) _____
(6) _____

Activity 2 Acquire Serving Skills

A The serving skills—8 hotel guest communication tips

Be proactive.
Be responsive.

Establish a regular communication.

Provide personalized communication and authentic interactions.

Encourage good reviews.

Be available and keep lines of communication open.

Monitor guest satisfaction during their stay.

B The details of establishing good hotel guest communication

1. Know what your guests want out of their stay, and then take it to the next level by exceeding their expectations. Anticipate the guests' needs by finding out why they're staying with you.

2. Respond quickly to complaints and negative comments, but also good ones. It's crucial that you or someone on your team interacts with your online followers in real-time to make a personal connection.

3. Each interaction with the guests—whether it's before they book their stay, during, or after they leave—should be infused with personalization and authenticity.

C Special tip

Whether you're an up-and-coming young professional or a seasoned manager, writing letter of acknowledgement is a vital aspect of business communication.

Sample:

> _____ Mr. Black,
>
> Thank you very much for _____ in Garden Hotel, and for your support and love for our Garden Hotel. We are very _____ to have you here. You can be equipped with a personal _____ to better serve you. Hotel staffs would make every _____ to provide the best service for you. If you have any comments or suggestions during your stay, please contact us.
>
> Any respectable guest is our most precious _____, and always take the needs of guests as our _____. Thank you again for choosing to stay in Garden Hotel, Happy New Year!
>
> Yours sincerely,
Demi
Customer Service Manager

Module 5 Other Hotel Service其他酒店服务

Activity 3 Practical Training

A Receive the tasks—role play

Task 1. Booking an Appointment

You are a customer service representative. You are phoning Mr. Black for an appointment. You would like to visit him on Tuesday morning. But he will have a meeting at that time. So you reschedule to Wednesday afternoon, which is OK to Mr. Black.

Task 2. Recommending Food

You are receiving an Russian client of your hotel who would like to try some Chinese food. The Russian client is on a business trip to Beijing. You would illustrate difference between Chinese and Western eating habits and preference.

Useful expressions

- Can you recommend a good Chinese restaurant?
- Do you have any other idea?
- For more causal dining, you could try the…
- There's always the…, where you can…
- I am calling to make an appointment with…
- I am sorry that…

B Training card

Name:	Class:	Date:
Your role:	Partner's role:	
Your task:		
Your process:		

(continue)

Conversation between the your partner and you.

Activity 4 Evaluate Your Study

No.	Tasks	Self-assessment	Group assessment	Teacher evaluation
1	I can tell the goals of visiting customers.			
2	I can tell the procedure of making appointment and food recommending.			
3	I can fill in a hotel feedback form.			
4	I can tell the details of building up a business relationship.			
5	I can master the vocabularies and expressions on customer visiting.			

Scene 4 Guest Service

Activity 1 Activate Language Knowledge

A Look at the pictures related to guest service, write down the correct vocabulary or phrases as quickly as possible

(1)_____

(2)_____

(3)_____

144

Module 5 Other Hotel Service 其他酒店服务

(4) _____

(5) _____

(6) _____

B Scan the QR code and listen to the conversation

Guest: Good morning, sir.

Receptionist: How may I help you?

Guest: I would like to book a flight ticket to Beijing. Can you book that for me?

Receptionist: Sure. For what time, please?

Guest: I would like to fly to Beijing this Saturday.

Receptionist: Let me see. Yes, there are three flights: 9:45 am, 11:45 am and 2:45 pm.

Guest: The one at 2:45 pm, please.

Receptionist: All right, could I have your passport and room card, please.

Guest: There you go.

Receptionist: Thank you. First class or economy class?

Guest: Economy class, please. How much is it?

Receptionist: It is 2300 RMB, with 10% discount, including airport construction fee and fuel additional fee.

Guest: OK. Thank you very much.

Receptionist: It is my pleasure.

扫码听音频

Task 1. Discussion with classmates

1. Where would he like to go?
2. Does the guest need to show the passport?
3. When is the flight departure's time?

Task 2. Practice with teammates

Write down the sequence of booking flight ticket?

(1) show the passport   (2) confirm the price

(3) state the destination   (4) confirm the flight time

C Read the passage on "Lost & Found"

If there's one customer service that hotels generally tend to overlook, it's probably lost and found.

But the fact is that lost and found truly does deserve every hotel's consideration because it can hugely affect brand loyalty and customer satisfaction. Guests lose things, it's something that happens frequently. However, just because it's a regular occurrence doesn't mean that the event of a lost guest item should be treated lightly.

According to research, a person can expect to lose or misplace as many as 3,000 times over the course of a lifetime. Does that mean that guests don't care about lost property? Absolutely not. So, where do you start? The best way to holistically analyze and improve your lost and found management process is by establishing clear protocols and procedures so that all of your staff members will know what they need to do when this type of issue arises.

Note

overlook	v.	忽略；未注意到；俯视；眺望
deserve	v.	应受；值得
loyalty	n.	忠诚；忠心
occurrence	n.	发生；事件；出现
treat	v.	对待；视为
misplace	v.	错放；误给
property	n.	财产；所有物
holistically	adv.	整体地；全盘地
arise	v.	出现

Decide whether the statements are true(T) or false(F) after reading.

(　　) 1. If there's one customer service that hotels generally tend to overlook, it's probably cleaning service.

(　　) 2. Lost and found truly does deserve every hotel's consideration because it can hugely affect customer satisfaction.

(　　) 3. Guests lose things, it's something that often happens.

(　　) 4. According to research, a person can expect to lose or misplace as many as 2,000 times over the course of a lifetime.

D Language tip

If 引导的条件从句，结构为：if+陈述句，主语+谓语。

1. 主句为一般将来时，if 引导的条件状语从句常用一般现在时。（主将从现）

　　例句：Please call me if he comes back.

2. 主句有情态动词 can, may, must, need 等时，从句常用一般现在时。（主情从现）

　　例句：You should see a doctor if you have a fever.

3. 主句为祈使句时，从句常用一般现在时。（主祈从现）

　　例句：If it doesn't rain tomorrow, we will go to have a picnic in the park.

Fill in the blanks with the given words.

1. If you _____ (come) to the party tomorrow, you _____ (have) a great time.
2. If you _____ (work) hard, you _____ (success).
3. If you want to _____ (lose) weight, you must _____ (eat) less bread.
4. If you _____ (not strong) enough, please _____ (not take part) in such an activity.
5. If he _____ (come), he _____ (tell) me all.

E Test yourself

Task 1. put the sentences into the right order. The first one has been done for you.

(1) Good afternoon, sir. What can I do for you?

(   ) There you go.

(   ) The flight at 9:45 am is China Southen. Is if OK for you?

(   ) First class, please. How much is it?

(   ) All right, could I have your passport and room card, please.

(   ) I would like to book a flight ticket to Guangzhou on October 17th. Can you book that for me?

(   ) It is my pleasure.

(   ) It is 9300 RMB, with 10% discount, including airport construction fee and fuel additional fee.

(   ) That will be fine.

(   ) Let me see. Yes, there are three flights: 9:45 am, 11:45 am and 2:45 pm. What time do you prefer?

(   ) The one at 9:45 am, please.

(   ) What class do you prefer? First class or economy class?

(   ) OK. Thank you very much.

Task 2. Scan the QR code and interpret what you hear from Chinese into English or from English into Chinese.

扫码听音频

(1)_____

(2)_____

(3)_____

(4)_____

(5)_____

(6)_____

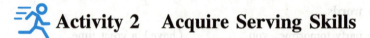
Activity 2 Acquire Serving Skills

A The serving skills—dealing with lost and found

Step one: Address the guests properly.
Step two: Check your hotel Lost and Found.
Step three: File an Lost and Found report, including the guest's name, the guest's reservation and contact information, a description of the item, the last time the item was seen, when the item was reported missing.
Step four: Confirm Circumstances.
Step five: Perform Your Own Investigation.
Step six: Talk to Relevant Staff Members.

B The details of dealing with lost & found

1. If an item is found, take it to the dedicated lost and found location in your hotel as soon as they are found.
2. If you have permission to access this area, make sure that you secure the item under lock and key when you have delivered it.
3. Report finding a lost item into a housekeeping software.
4. The software will automatically add all relevant details (such as location, guest information, date and time, etc.).
5. Put each item in a separate plastic bag before storing.
6. All valuable items (phones, wallets, tablets, computers, jewelry) should be stored in a secure locker.
7. If it's a non-valuable item, it stays in lost and found for two months if no one retrieves it and then discarded.
8. If it's a perishable item (like food), it can be discarded after three days if no one claims it.

C Special tip

A memo, short for *memorandum*, is a way to inform a group of people about a specific problem, solution, or event. A memo should be brief, straightforward, and easy to read. It informs recipients and provides an action plan with specific next steps. The following purposes are suitable for a memo: broadcast internal changes, disseminate news, share an upcoming event, update public safety guidelines, raise awareness about an issue, address a problem, make a request, share project updates.

Sample:

> **Memo**
>
> From: Boni Mansi, Director of Operations
> To: All Staffs and guests
> Date: 4th January, 2023
> Subject: Maintenance Work
>
>   Please be advised that there will be a schedule maintenance work on our swimming pool on the 7th till 28th January, 2023, during this time the swimming pool will be totally closed for guest usage. The swimming pool will be open for guest usage on 29th January 2023 as per the normal operating time.

Activity 3 Practical Training

A Receive the tasks—role play.

Task 1. Leaving a message

You are the receptionist, John. Mr Black calls to leave a message to Mr. White, whose room number is 1666. Mr. Black would like to know the budget report and progress of the new project. Mr. Black hopes Mr. White can call him back when he is back. Mr. Black's phone number is 888666999.

Task 2. Ordering service

You are a customer service representative. Mr. White phones you to help him buy some souvenirs as business gifts. He hopes not to buy too expensive gifts but choose high-quality products as business gift. The budget is around 200 RMB. The souvenir should reflect the Cantonese culture.

Useful expressions

- I would like to leave a message to…
- Is there a number where you can be reached.
- OK, I will make sure he/she gets your message.
- Could you please help me with buying…
- What is your requirement?
- What is your budget?

B Training card

Name:	Class:	Date:
Your role:	Partner's role:	
Your task:		
Your process:		

Conversation between the guest (your partner) and the housemaid (you).

Activity 4 Evaluate Your Study

No.	Tasks	Self-assessment	Group assessment	Teacher evaluation
1	I can tell how to order things for customers.			
2	I can tell the procedure of dealing with "Lost & Found".			
3	I can leave a message to the guests.			
4	I can tell the details of giving business gifts.			
5	I can master vocabularies and expressions on "Lost & Found" service.			

Module 5 Other Hotel Service其他酒店服务

Chinese Story

Chinese Traditional Costume

China Bouquet—Traditional Chinese Costume in Modern Times

"China's rituals and etiquette make Chinese people who they are, and their beautiful clothes make them glorious".

China has been known as "a state of ceremonies" and "a well-dressed country" since ancient times. During those eras, traditional costume defined Chinese culture. The shape, structure, patterns and colors of clothes and accessories were not just a matter of regime, functions and aesthetics; moreover, it reflected China's history, culture and values.

"Hanfu", also known as "Han Costume", is more than clothes and accessories from the Han Dynasty. It encompasses the entire dress code and clothing system of the traditional Han ethnic group. A complete set of hats, and clothing were formed during Han Dynasty based on the Four Books and Five Classics. Traditional Chinese costume conveys the characteristics of the Han ethnic group, which is quiet and balanced. Their aesthetic taste is simple, natural, implicit and mild.

Today, designers have worked to reproduce traditional Chinese costume that is better suited for modern people. Some summarized the core of Hanfu, while others continued to use the traditional ways. Some artists even created crossover artworks with Hanfu elements.

A. Write down the names of minority group of their traditional costume.

(1) _____

(2) _____

(3) _____

(4) _____ (5) _____ (6) _____

(7) _____ (8) _____ (9) _____

B. Work in pairs. Discuss the costume you may find in different dynasties.

Periods	Costumes	Features
Han Dynasty		
Tang Dynasty		
Yuan Dynasty		
Ming Dynasty		
Qing Dynasty		
Republic of China Era		

C. Work in Team.

① For celebrating the splendid Winter Olympic Game held in Beijing, you and your friends decide to introduce one of Chinese traditional costume for the athletes.

Module 5   Other Hotel Service其他酒店服务

Choose a representative from each group to report the costume and the reason you wanting to introduce this Chinese costume to the athletes.

Module 6

Interview
面 试

? Questions for thinking

1. What is your future plan after graduation?
2. Can you list some positions in the hotel?

Goals

After studying this project, you should be able to:

√ Know about some famous hotels.
√ Write a resume.
√ Know how to prepare an interview.
√ Know how to take part in an interview.

Prepare for learning

Scan the following QR code to learn the new words and take a test on ***. You can begin the learning of this module if your test score is over 70.

扫码听音频

Scene 1　Get to Know Hotel and Yourself

Activity 1　Activate Language Knowledge

A Look at the icons of different place around city, write down the Chinese names accordingly

(1)＿＿＿＿＿　　(2)＿＿＿＿＿　　(3)＿＿＿＿＿

(4)＿＿＿＿＿　　(5)＿＿＿＿＿　　(6)＿＿＿＿＿

(7)＿＿＿＿＿　　(8)＿＿＿＿＿　　(9)＿＿＿＿＿

(7)＿＿＿＿＿　　(8)＿＿＿＿＿　　(9)＿＿＿＿＿

B Scan the QR code and listen to the conversation

Susan: Good morning everyone. Welcome to our hotel. My name is Susan, the HR manager in our hotel. It is my honor to be here to show you around and introduce our hotel brand. If you have any questions, please feel free to ask me.

扫码听音频

Visitor: You are so nice, Susan. May I know something about the hotel history?

Susan: Sure. The hotel was established in the United States in 1928. By the close of 1992, it had expanded to 23 exceptional luxury hotels. The following year, we opened the first hotel in Asia, The W-Hotel, Hong Kong.

Visitor: It is a wonderful hotel brand. What is the service standard of The R-Hotel?

Susan: Our hotel is a luxury hotel which earned its first Malcolm Baldrige National Quality Award in 1993.

Visitor: Wow, it sounds good. How many rooms are there in this hotel?

Susan: There are 351 rooms in our hotel including executive suites with the lounge. And the facilities and services of our hotel are superb. I'll show you around the leisure area. This way, please.

Visitor: Thank you very much.

Task 1. Discussion with classmates

1. Who is introducing the hotel?
2. When was The Ritz-Carlton established?
3. What is the service standard of The Ritz-Carlton hotel?

Task 2. Practice with teammates

Try to find out what key information we have known about the company.

1. The name of the hotel: _____
2. The products and services it offers: _____
3. The achievements of the company: _____
4. Other information that you think is important: _____

C Read the passage on White Swan Hotel

The **iconic** five-star city-resort in the historic heart of Guangzhou.

Majestically overlooking the scenic Pearl River from its location on historic Shamian Island, the White Swan Hotel is an **oasis** of **tranquility** amid the **hustle** and **bustle** of the city. As a welcoming entrance, the impressive Atrium lobby is an indoor **microcosm** of the lush landscapes of southern China with a cascading waterfall over spectacular rockery.

First opened in 1983, the White Swan Guangzhou is

Note

iconic *adj.* 偶像的，图符的，象征性的
majestically *adv.* 雄伟地，庄严地；威严地
oasis *n.* (沙漠中的)绿洲
tranquility *n.* 宁静，安宁
hustle *n.* 忙碌，熙熙攘攘
bustle *n.* 喧闹，繁忙
microcosm *n.* 微观世界；小宇宙

one of the most recognized five star luxury hotels in China and a member of the "World Luxury Collection" by World hotels. Over the years, the hotel has received many heads of states, including Queen Elizabeth II, and is renowned for extending exceptional service to every guest.

As White Swan Hotel is newly renovated, the hotel in Guangzhou features 520 luxurious rooms and suites, over 2500 square meters of well appointed meeting and conference space, a two-level fitness center, a heated outdoor pool, an exclusive Spa sanctuary, designer shops, and a variety of excellent restaurants, bars and lounges.

landscape　*n.*（陆上，尤指乡村的）风景，景色
cascade　*v.*（水）倾泻，流注
spectacular　*adj.* 壮观的，令人惊叹的
renowned　*adj.* 有名望的，著名的
exceptional　*adj.* 卓越的，杰出的；不寻常的，罕见的
lounge　*n.* 酒廊

Decide whether the statements are true(T) or false(F) after reading.

(　　) 1. White Swan Hotel is an economy hotel.
(　　) 2. White Swan Hotel is on the bank of Pearl River.
(　　) 3. The hotel was firstly opened in 1980s.
(　　) 4. The hotel hasn't be renovated since it was opened.

D Language tip

表示将来时态：will/be going to/be doing。
1. 表示将来计划做某事时，强调意图+计划或者预测，用 be going to.
　　例句：I am going to meet Tom at the station at six.（有计划）
2. 表示最近将来的确定安排，强调已经事先做好准备，用 be doing.
　　例句：I am meeting Tom at the station at six.（有计划并约好）
3. will 表示临时想去做什么或者决心，只有意图没有计划，并且只用于第一人称。
　　例句：I will help you.

Choose the correct verbs to complete the sentences.

1. I _____ Tom in the restaurant at six. We want to give him a big surprise.（be going to meet/be meeting）
2. A：There is somebody at the door.
　　B：I _____ go and open it.（be going to /will）
3. We _____ together this winter.（be going to go skiing/be going skiing）
4. A：Why is he carrying his guitar?
　　B：He _____ play it in the underground.（will/be going to）
5. Look at those clouds. It _____ rain.（will/be going to）

Module 6 Interview面试

E Test yourself

Task 1. Put the sentences into the right order. The first one has been done for you.

(1) What are your plans for the future, Amy?
(   ) That's true. So I think we had better get more certificates in the school.
(   ) Well, my short-term goal is to pass all my exams at the end of this semester.
(   ) I think so, but the work experience is also important, which will be helpful for job hunting.
(   ) Me too! But recently I've started to think of long-term goals. You know, I really want to get a good job.
(   ) Absolutely right!
(   ) I've been thinking about that too. Outstanding graduates have much wider opportunities to choose from.

Task 2. Scan the QR code and interpret what you hear from Chinese into English or from English into Chinese.

(1) _____
(2) _____
(3) _____
(4) _____
(5) _____
(6) _____

Activity 2   Acquire Career Planning Skills

A The career planning skills—job research

Step one: Study or work? Make a decision.
Step two: Job hunting.
Step three: Do some company research.
Step four: Prepare a resume.
Step five: Write and send an application letter together with your resume.
Step six: Take part in the interview.
Step seven: Accept the offer.

B The details when applying for a job

1. Know a company before a job interview is very important.
2. Get detailed information about a company is crucial to job applicants.

3. Do some rehearsals before taking part in the interview.

4. Don't forget to write a thanks letter to the persons who gave you help after interview.

5. Be polite and confident.

C Tips for writing a job application letter

1. **Use business letter format.** Include your contact information at the top, the date, and the employer's contact information.

2. **Use keywords.** Reread the job listing, circling any keywords (such as skills or abilities). Try to include some of those words in your cover letter.

3. **Keep it brief.** Keep your letter under a page long, with no more than about four paragraphs.

4. **Proofread and edit.** Read through your cover letter, and if possible, ask a friend or career counselor to review the letter. Proofread for any grammar or spelling errors.

Sample:

Dear HR manager,

  I found the position advertised on your company's website. I am writing this letter in hope of applying for this job in your hotel.

  I will graduate in June, major in Business English. I have a good command of Business English and the basic theory of public relationship. My experience of working with others has give me confidence in my interpersonal skills and decision-making abilities. The enclosed resume outlines my credential and accomplishment in detail.

  I learn about your hotel, which is renowned for its excellent management. I also appreciate the culture of your company. I sincerely hope you give me an opportunity to get a new challenge in your company.

  I am available for an interview at any time convenient to you. Looking forward to your early reply.

B. RGS

Activity 3   Practical Training

A Receive the task—role play

Task 1: Giving job hunting advice

  John is a career supervisor in the HR department. He is very warm-hearted and always eager to solve students' various problems on career choices. Now he is giving suggestions to you, a student majored in hotel management, about how to apply for a job.

Task 2: Giving suggestions on job interview

Ton is a student majored in hotel management. He has taken a lot of job interviews, but all failed. John, a HR manager in a hotel, is giving Tom suggestions on job interview.

Useful expressions

- What position are you interested in?
- ... company will recruit on our campus this weekend.
- Fantastic! I hear it's a great company to work for.
- A receptionist answers phones and takes messages.
- Do you think I should take anything to the recruitment event?
- I think you should take an up-to-date copy of your resume.

B Training card

Name:	Class:	Date:
Your role:	Partner's role:	
Your task:		
Your process:		
Conversation between the career supervisor (your partner) and the graduate (you).		

Activity 4   Evaluate Your Study

No.	Tasks	Self-assessment	Group assessment	Teacher evaluation
1	I can recognize some world-famous hotel brand.			

(continue)

No.	Tasks	Self-assessment	Group assessment	Teacher evaluation
2	I can tell my decision after graduation.			
3	I can tell the details of job searching.			
4	I can write an application letter.			
5	I can master vocabularies and expressions on preparation for job searching.			

Scene 2　　Interview Criteria

Activity 1　Activate Language Knowledge

A Look at the pictures related to job searching, write down the correct vocabulary accordingly

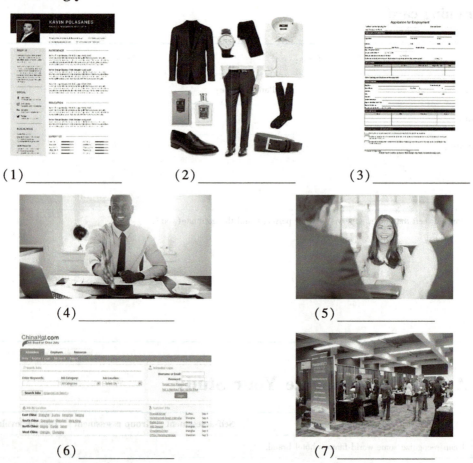

(1) ＿＿＿＿＿＿　　(2) ＿＿＿＿＿＿　　(3) ＿＿＿＿＿＿

(4) ＿＿＿＿＿＿　　(5) ＿＿＿＿＿＿

(6) ＿＿＿＿＿＿　　(7) ＿＿＿＿＿＿

Module 6　Interview面试

B　Scan the QR code and listen to the conversation

扫码听音频

Interviewer：Well, your resume looks terrific. Do you have any related work experience?

Candidate：I interned as an assistant at a shipping company during my last three months.

Interviewer：What capabilities do you have that you believe would make you successful here?

Candidate：I'm always curious about everything. Ever since I started my major, I have been completely indulged in it.

Interviewer：Let's talk about the compensation. What kind of salary are you hoping for?

Candidate：It is impossible to give an exact number. 3,500 to 4,000 RMB per month?

Interviewer：I've got to tell you our base rate for this position is 3,000 RMB per month, but if we are really satisfied with your performance, I think it is open for further discussion.

Candidate：Well, I'd like to be paid a salary that reflects the current standard for my vacancy.

Interviewer：OK, I also hope to have the chance to get to know you better in the future.

Candidate：Thank you for your time. I am looking forward to the next interview.

Task 1. Discussion with classmates

1. What do you consider as your weaknesses?

2. What is your greatest strength?

3. How much do you expect for your salary?

Task 2. Practice with teammates

Play a Question & Answer game with your partner according to the dialogue.

(1) work experience

(2) capabilities

(3) salary

C　Read the passage on interview

In common parlance, the word "interview" refers to a one-on-one conversation between an interviewer and an interviewee. This feature is common to many types of interviews. A job interview is a meeting between a job candidate and an interviewer, who is typically a manager, human resources personnel, another representative of the employer or the employer. This meeting is held to help assess whether the applicant is the right person for the role.

Note

parlance　n. 说法；用语；
　　　　　　语调；发言

interviewer　n. 面试官

interviewee　n. 参加面试者

163

While not every hiring process will contain the same elements and each interview will be specific to the job, there are certain things that you can expect of the interview format so that you can arrive prepared for the experience. The average interview usually progresses through basic stages including the following:

personnel	n.	人事
assess	v.	评估
element	n.	基本部分, 要素; 元素
format	n.	总体安排, 计划, 设计

1. Introduction

To give a good first impression, make sure that you make eye contact, shake their hand firmly and say something like, "Hi, it's so nice to meet you."

2. Question and Answer

Depending on the company and industry, you can experience different types of interview questions.

3. Concluding the interview

At the end of your interview, you should shake the interviewer's hand and thank them for their time and consideration. Remember to make eye contact and smile.

Decide whether the statements are true(T) or false(F) after reading.

( ) 1. All the interviews have the same purpose.

( ) 2. You can answer the questions you like during the interview.

( ) 3. At the interviews end, you had better not shake hands with the manager.

( ) 4. Generally the interview refers to the conversation between the interviewer and the interviewee.

D Language tip

would like 和 want 的用法:

1. 用于邀请时我们用 would you like 而不用 Do you want? 后者只是问句而不是邀请，前者通常要比后者有礼貌些。

2. 在否定式中 would like 有别于 want。

don't want = have no wish for(不想)，而 wouldn't like = would dislike(不喜欢)。因此 wouldn't like 不能用来回答别人的邀请或建议，因为这样不礼貌。

Choose the correct answer to complete the sentences.

1. **Would you like/Do you want** to go to the theatre?

2. —Would you like some more coffee?

 —No, I **wouldn't like/don't want** any more, thanks.

3. Mr. Smith is out. **Would you like/Do you want** to leave a message?

4. Tom said he **would have liked/wanted to** see it.

5. I **would like to/want to** have gone.

E Test yourself

Task 1. Put the sentences into the right order. The first one has been done for you.

(1) Hi, Sam. What are you doing?

(   ) Maybe you need to have a really great resume.

(   ) That's true. Many hotels and restaurants are not willing to offer job vacancies.

(   ) Job hunting! You know, the employment situation is still grim this year.

(   ) You are right. I should polish my resume and prepare for the interview.

(   ) More than 10, but no reply till now.

(   ) How many application letters have you sent?

(   ) I wish you good luck.

(   ) Thank you. I'm job hunting.

Task 2. Scan the QR code and interpret what you hear from Chinese into English or from English into Chinese.

(1) _____

(2) _____

(3) _____

(4) _____

(5) _____

(6) _____

Activity 2 Acquire Interview Skills

A The Interview skills—interview procedure

Step one: How to Preparing for an interview?

　　　　　research the organization.

　　　　　prepare and practice your answer.

　　　　　calm your nerves.

　　　　　polish your image.

Step two: During the interview.

　　　　　Make a good first impression.

　　　　　Answer the right questions.

　　　　　Ask questions.

　　　　　Get your tone right.

　　　　　Pay attention to your body language.

Step three: After the interview.
　　　　　　Follow-up.
　　　　　　Get the feedback.

B The details when you get the chance for interview

1. Preparation is essential before an interview. Research the company, prepare answers for likely questions, plan your journey, and role-play your performance. If you're struggling with confidence, take the time to invest in yourself and learn techniques to keep your cool.

2. During the interview, try to make a good first impression, pay close attention to your tone and body language and ask questions. Listen attentively to make sure you're answering exactly what you're being asked. Your first interview may not be the best time to ask about salary and benefits. These can be difficult issues to discuss.

3. Once the interview is over, send a thank-you message to everyone involved in the process. Whether you secure the position or not, ask for feedback to learn from the experience and to improve your interview skills for the future.

C Special tip

The interview may indeed be the bulk of the process, but when the interview ends you still have an opportunity to make an impression. After each interview during the interview process, you should send a <u>follow-up email</u> to the person you met with. Make sure to:

- Thank them again for meeting with you.
- Take a second to clarify or ask anything that you wish you had during the interview.
- Reiterate your eagerness to join their team.

Sample:

Activity 3　Practical Training

A　Receive the task—role play

Task 1.　Making interview dialogue 1

Employer card
Position: Hotel Receptionist
Skills required: computer skill, communication skill, English skill
Others: work experience, work overtime, salary etc.

Your name is Gao Min, a graduate student from Guangdong University of Foreign Studies. You are applying for a position of hotel receptionist. Your interviewer, Mr. Chen is interviewing you.

Task 2.　Making interview dialogue 2

Employer card
Position: Reservations Agent
Skills required: computer skill, marketing skill, communication skill, English skill
Others: work experience, work overtime, salary etc.

Your name is Li Lin, a graduate student from Guangdong University of Hotel and Restaurant Management. You are applying for a position of reservations agent. Your interviewer, Mr. Yan is interviewing you.

Useful expressions

- What kind of personality do you think you have?
- What sort of work experience do you have?
- What are your qualifications?
- I am hard-working, outgoing and friendly.
- I am good at office software, and I have some basic knowledge of doing business with foreigners.
- I work as an assistant at the Canton Fair last two years.

B Training card

Name:	Class:	Date:
Your role:		Partner's role:
Your task:		
Your process:		
Conversation between the interviewer (your partner) and the jobseeker (you).		

Activity 4 Evaluate Your Study

No.	Tasks	Self-assessment	Group assessment	Teacher evaluation
1	I can tell the details of preparation before interview.			
2	I can tell the details of interview procedure.			
3	I can tell how to deal with the interview.			
4	I can tell how to write a follow-up letter.			
5	I can master vocabularies and expressions on interviews.			

Module 6 Interview 面试

Scene 3   English Resume

Activity 1   Activate Language Knowledge

A Look at the pictures about resumes, write down the correct vocabulary accordingly

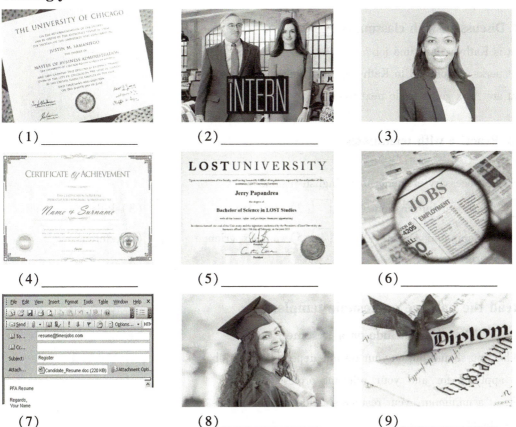

(1) _____   (2) _____   (3) _____

(4) _____   (5) _____   (6) _____

(7) _____   (8) _____   (9) _____

B Scan the QR code and listen to the conversation

扫码听音频

Alex: Hi, Kathy! Where are you going?
Kathy: Hi, Alex! I'm just on my way to work.
Alex: Congratulations! Where are you working?
Kathy: I've just got a part-time job as a receptionist in a hotel.
Alex: Great! What are your hours like?
Kathy: I work on Tuesday and Thursday evenings and Sundays too.
Alex: Ah, so you can fit your work around your studies. That's good.

169

Kathy: Yeah, it suits me really well. I hope I can get a job in this hotel after graduation.
Alex: And what's the work like? Do you enjoy it?
Kathy: Yeah, I do. It's a nice place to work and my colleagues are friendly.
Alex: Do you get any perks?
Kathy: I get free entry to the gym and to the swimming pool too. What about you? Do you have your resume ready?
Alex: Yes, I have already well-prepared to take part in an interview next week.
Kathy: Good luck! Look forward to your good news.

Task1. Discussion with classmates

1. What is Kathy's part-time job?
2. What perks are offered to Kathy by the hotel?
3. What are Alex going to do next week?

Task 2. Practice with teammates

Tick the necessary elements in a English resume.

☐ (1) personal Information ☐ (2) education ☐ (3) skills
☐ (4) honors and Awards ☐ (5) work Experience ☐ (6) references

C Read the passage on resume template

What Do I Include on a Resume?

What you should put on your resume depends on the job you're applying for and your relevant professional background. At a minimum, your resume should include the following sections:

Contact details: include your first and last name, phone number, and email address. Additionally, you can add your Linked In profile if yours is up to date.

Introduction: a concise overview of your professional background and key qualifications. Your introduction can be in the form of a resume summary, professional profile, resume objective, or qualifications summary.

Education: include your school names, highest degree earned, majors and minors. Additionally, you can add your

> **Note**
>
> profile *n.* 简介，概况

170

GPA (if it's greater than 3.8) and relevant coursework if you lack experience or it's related to the position.

Experience: list any relevant work experience you have. Include your title, the company you worked for, years worked, and a bulleted list of your key responsibilities and notable successes. Be sure to also include as many relevant accomplishments on your resume as possible.

Skills: include any resume skills you possess that are relevant to the position. Be sure to use a strong mix of hard skills and soft skills to demonstrate that you're a well-rounded candidate.

GPA (grade point average)
　　　　　　　adj. 平均绩点
relevant　　*adj.* 相关的
coursework　*n.* 修习，职业培训
bulleted list　上面的列表中列出
notable　*adj.* 显著的，值得注意的
accomplishment　*n.* 成就，业绩，素养
demonstrate　*v.* 证明，示范
well-rounded　*adj.* 丰满的，面面俱到的

Decide whether the statements are true(T) or false(F) after reading.

(　　) 1. You should introduce your education from your kindergarten.
(　　) 2. You can create a long list in your resume.
(　　) 3. You should add some resume skills you possess that are relevant to the position.
(　　) 4. Part time jobs are not included in your work experience.

D Language tip

can 和 be able

时态	肯定式	否定式	疑问式
现在时	can/am able	can't/am not able	can I? /am I able?
过去时	could/was able	could not/was not able	could I? /was I able?
将来时	I will/shall able 或者 he/she will be able	I will/shall not be able 或者 he/she will not be able	will/shall I be able? 或者 will he/she be able?

1. can 和 am able 都可用于现在时，can 更常用。
2. could 和 was able 表示过去能力，两者可用，但表示能力+特定行为，要用 was able。
3. 将来时只有一个形式。

Choose the correct verbs to complete the sentences.

1. **Could you/Were you able to** show me the way?
2. Although the pilot was badly hurt he **could/was able to** explain what had happened.
3. I **could/was able to** have lent you the money. Why didn't you ask me?
4. My baby **can/will be able to** walk in a few weeks.

5. Since his accident he **couldn't/hasn't been able to** leave the house.

E Test yourself

Task 1. Put the education information in the resume into the right order.
The first one has been done for you.

(1) Hi Cherry, have you heard the news?
(   ) Front desk. What about you?
(   ) I think I would like to work in housekeeper section.
(   ) What kind of position would you like to ben after?
(   ) Really? I heard it is a great hotel to work for.
(   ) Well, White Swan Hotel is holding a recruitment drive on campus this weekend.
(   ) No, what's happening?
(   ) Well, I am going to take an up-to-date copy of my resume.
(   ) Good idea.

Task 2. Scan the QR code and interpret what you hear from Chinese into English or from English into Chinese.

扫码听音频

(1) _____
(2) _____
(3) _____
(4) _____
(5) _____
(6) _____

Activity 2   Acquire Writing Skills

A The writing skills—writing a resume procedure

Step one: Choose a resume format.

Step two: Add your name and contact information.

Step three: Write a standout resume headlines.

Step four: Add your professional resume summary statement.

Step five: Detail your work experience.

Step six: List relevant skills and keywords.

Step seven: Add your education, certifications and other relevant information.

Step eight: Tailor your resume and optimize for applicant tracking systems.

Step nine: Polish up your grammar and formatting.

B The details when writing a resume

1. Add a personal phone number, never a work number.
2. Mention your most impressive achievements. Bonus points for using numbers and specifics.
3. It's important to use a font that is easy to read on screen, ATS-compatible and commonly available. Avoid using script fonts or custom fonts unless you are a designer. Don't use a font size below 10.
4. Use past tense when talking about jobs in the past, and present tense when describing the work you are currently doing. Traditional resume writing leaves out personal pronouns (I) and gets right to the action. Ex. "Spearheaded a new email marketing initiative that increased revenue by 10 percent."
5. Action verbs help liven up your writing, making your resume more readable for recruiters and hiring managers. Consider beginning each bullet point on your resume with an action verb and replacing generic verbs like "managed" or "led" with more engaging words like "mentored" or "accelerated".

C Special tip

A resume headline is a concise, one-line description of who you are as a candidate. A well-written headline can grab a recruiter's attention and encourage them to take a more detailed look at your qualifications. Your headline is a short but powerful addition to your resume, often the first thing a recruiter reads.

Sample:

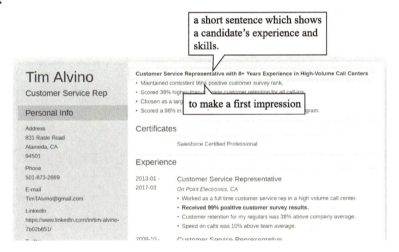

Activity 3   Practical Training

A Receive the tasks—role play

Task 1. Job seeker

You are a graduate student. You are applying for a post of Hotel Receptionist in a company. And you should prepare a resume before the interview.

Task 2. Job discussion

You are a graduate student. You are going to apply for room attendant in a hotel. You are discussing your job plan with your roommate.

Useful expressions

- Majored in/minored in…
- Worked as…
- Passed CET 6 at college
- Be passionate and sincere, good public relationship, good at communicating with different kinds of people
- Be hard-working with sense of responsibility, adaptability and willingness to rise to the challenges
- Self-motivated, good planning ability and can travel frequently, target-oriented and good service attitude

B Training card

Name:	Class:	Date:
Your role:		Partner's role:
Your task:		
Your process:		

Write your own resume/CV with the help of the above notes.

Activity 4 Evaluate Your Study

No.	Tasks	Self-assessment	Group assessment	Teacher evaluation
1	I can tell the difference of a resume and a CV.			
2	I can tell the main elements of a resume.			
3	I can tell the details of a resume.			
4	I can write a resume.			
5	I can master vocabularies and expressions on resume.			

Scene 4   Orientation

Activity 1 Activate Language Knowledge

A Look at the pictures of orientation, write down the correct vocabulary accordingly

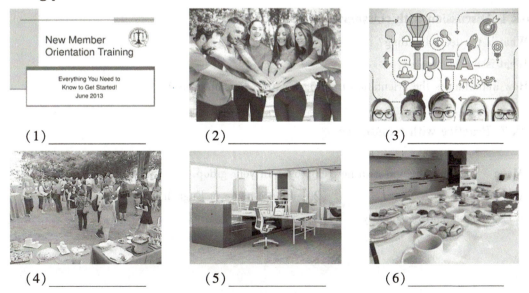

(1)＿＿＿＿＿＿   (2)＿＿＿＿＿＿   (3)＿＿＿＿＿＿

(4)＿＿＿＿＿＿   (5)＿＿＿＿＿＿   (6)＿＿＿＿＿＿

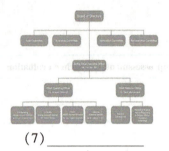  

(7) ＿＿＿＿＿＿　　(8) ＿＿＿＿＿＿　　(9) ＿＿＿＿＿＿

B Scan the QR code and listen to the conversation

扫码听音频

Vivian: Welcome to this team building workshop! Over this weekend, you'll have the opportunity to get to know your co-workers better.

Participant: OK, we are ready. How to run it?

Vivian: Your team is made up of new comers from different sections. Getting to know your co-workers, and helping them get to know each other, will build an efficient and trusting team. The workshop aims to encourage everyone to work well together as a team by participating in different kinds of activities. I hope you can learn to build a team based on everyone's strengths and weaknesses.

Participant: Sounds great! So what shall we do now?

Vivian: At first, we are going to have an icebreaker to get everyone warmed up. Later and tomorrow, we'll have various activities including a guess game, a personality test and company culture introduction. I hope you can enjoy it.

Participant: Sure.

Task 1. Discussion with classmates

1. What is the team building?

2. What is the icebreaker?

3. How important is the orientation training for the new employees?

Task 2. Practice with teammates

> Make a self-introduction as a new employee in your group.
>
> (1) opening　　　　　　　　(2) chinese name & English name
>
> (3) interests and personality　　(4) ending

C Read the passage on orientation

Orientation training for new employees is the process of introducing new hires to their job tasks, company processes, and teams. But it's also the beginning of a relationship between the employee and their employer. Like any relationship, a shaky start usually leads to an imminent end.

Many companies view orientation as an administrative process, where employees become familiar with the rules, sign their contracts, and get to work. You can almost imagine a manager striking off items from their imaginary new employee orientation checklist, proudly thinking that another demanding task is done. The truth is there's a lot more to orientation. The real purpose of new hire orientation is to mentally and emotionally integrate employees into the organization, and equip them with the skills, tools, and support they need to reach their potential.

Because with every new hire who joins your company, it's safe to assume that they want to make a meaningful contribution, that they'd like to feel loyal to their team, and that you should give them all the resources they need to succeed. If these assumptions are difficult to make, chances are that you've made some mistakes in the hiring process.

Note

orientation	n.	岗前培训，迎新
shaky	adj.	不牢靠的
imminent	adj.	即将发生的
administrative	adj.	行政的
checklist	n.	清单；检查表
mentally	adj.	精神上，智力上；心理上
integrate	v.	合并，融合
assume	v.	假定，假设

Decide whether the statements are true (T) or false (F) after reading.

( ) 1. Orientation training is also the beginning of a relationship between the employee and their employer.

( ) 2. New hires don't want to make a meaningful contribution.

( ) 3. There must be some mistakes if your new hires wouldn't like to feel loyal to their team.

( ) 4. The real purpose of new hire orientation is to physically integrate employees into the organization.

D Language tip

if 和 in case

1. in case 引出的从句为主句行动的理由，可以省略掉而不改变主句的含义。如果省略掉 if 从句，主句含义发生变化。

> 例句：I'll come tomorrow in case Ann wants me. （我明天一定去）
>
> I'll come tomorrow if Ann wants me. （安明天去，我才去）
>
> 2. in case of +名词=if there is a/an +名词
>
> 例句：In case of accident, phone 999. = If there is an accident, phone 999.

Choose the correct word to complete the sentences.

1. I always slept by the phone **if/in case** he rang during the night.
2. **If/In case** we were not back by midnight, we'll be locked out.
3. I'll carry a spare wheel **if/in case** I have a puncture.
4. I don't let him climb trees **if/in case** he tears his trousers.
5. **If/In case** you like, I'll get a ticket for you.

E Test yourself

Task 1. Put the sentences into the right order. The first one has been done for you.

Team building occurs in eight stages:

(1) Hi Joe! What do you say about the team building workshop last weekend?

(   ) It was really an unforgettable experience.

(   ) Having fun was an important part of the workshop though. Besides, we had the chance to see another side of our co-workers.

(   ) The trust game. I think we've all got to learn to trust each other more in order to build a strong team. How about you?

(   ) Yeah, I guess you're right. What was your favorite game during the session?

(   ) My favourite part was the personality test.

(   ) I also love this part. It is so interesting.

(   ) Yes. I think everyone had a good time. But I don't know how much it helped us to be a better team.

Task 2. Scan the QR code and interpret what you hear from Chinese into English or from English into Chinese.

扫码听音频

(1) _____

(2) _____

(3) _____

(4) _____

(5) _____

(6) _____

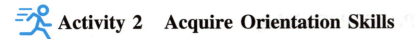

Activity 2 Acquire Orientation Skills

A The conducting skills—orientation procedure

Step one: Give employees a tour of the building/workplace.

Step two: Introduce them to key colleagues and supervisors/managers.

Step three: Get them set up with the necessary equipment.

Step four: Review their schedule.

Step five: Review initial project and expectation.

Step six: Conduct a team-building exercise.

Step seven: Introduce them to the employee handbook.

Step eight: Answer any questions they have.

B The details of an effective new employee orientation process

1. Put yourself in a new hire's shoes.
2. Create a single source of truth for new employees to reference.
3. Allow leadership to introduce themselves to new hires.
4. Break the ice with new hires.
5. Break up meetings.
6. Ask for feedback.

C Special tip

Undoubtedly, the new hire orientation process is very important for both employers and employees. Employers that make this orientation process seamless and stress-free will do a lot to make new employees feel welcome and comfortable. When building an effective new hire orientation format, some essential contents should be included.

Sample:

Orientation Format	
Content	Remark
The company, including history, mission, culture and current company wide goals.	
Organizational structure and department overviews.	
Benefit plans.	
Safety, health, and other company policies.	
Mandatory new hire paperwork.	
Administrative procedures, such as security, logins, available supplies, etc.	

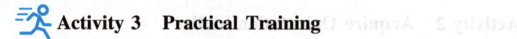

Activity 3　Practical Training

A　Receive the tasks—role play

Task 1. Find my friends

　　Now, please take a look at who is at the table with you. This is your chance to know more about your friends. I'll give you five minutes to find at least three new faces. You need to talk with them until you find something in common on jobs with each other, then form a team. You should introduce your teammates and explain the reason why you choose them.

Task 2. Blind drawing

　　Blind Drawing is a team-building activity that can be done in groups of 4 to 6. Each team must appoint one artist. Give the artist drawing materials and sit them with their back facing the rest of the team so they're not able to see the group. The group then picks an item or picture from those supplied. You must successfully get the artist to draw this item or picture in 3 minutes. However, you aren't allowed to tell the artist what the item is; you can only give indirect descriptions. When times up, groups should compare their drawings. It can be comical to see how badly they can turn out. The game can get people laughing and highlights how difficult giving instructions can be and how important it is to communicate clearly.

Useful expressions

- Do you accept the 996 work culture?
- Do you accept work far from home?
- Do you think teamwork is very important for you?
- What is your expectation on the first job salary?
- Do you think communication is crucial for a team?
- Do you accept changing jobs very often?

B　Training card

Name:	Class:	Date:
Your role:		Partner's role:
Your task:		
Your process:		

(continue)

Conversation between the teammates(your partner) and (you).

Activity 4　Evaluate Your Study

No.	Tasks	Self-assessment	Group assessment	Teacher evaluation
1	I can tell the importance of orientation.			
2	I can tell the details of orientation training.			
3	I can tell orientation procedure.			
4	I can tell something about team building, such as communication game, etc.			
5	I can master vocabularies and expressions on orientation.			

Chinese Story

Chinese Architecture

　　Ancient architecture varied greatly across civilizations, each with distinct styles and innovations. Egyptian architecture featured pyramids and temples. Greek architecture developed classical orders and emphasized symmetry in temples and public buildings. Chinese architecture used timber frames and curved roofs in palaces, following principles like feng shui. Each architecture reflected its cultural, religious, and technological achievements.

The main feature of traditional Chinese architecture has been its stability; styles did not change much over many centuries. In Europe, styles came in and out of fashion and so it is easy to guess the date of a building to within a century, this is not so easy in China.

Only a few of "ancient" buildings in China date back further than theMing dynasty due to their mainly wooden construction. Tourist sites that are described as "Han'" or "Tang" dynasty have in the main, although retaining the original design, been completely rebuilt in the last few centuries. Some of those that have survived intact include the Nanchan Temple; Foguang Temple, Shanxi (Wutai mountain) and there are also buildings of Tang dynasty date and design in Japan. China's architectural art is a particularly beautiful branch in the tree of Chinese civilization.

A. Write down the names of Chinese traditionalarchitecture

(1)_____   (2)_____   (3)_____

(4)_____   (5)_____   (6)_____

(7)_____   (8)_____   (9)_____

Module 6 Interview面试

B. Work in pairs. Discuss the architectures you may see in different cities.

Chinese architecture	Location	Description
Wuzhen Water Town		
Anji Bridge		
Yingxian Wooden Pogoda		
Yongding Hakka Tulou		
Shikumen Dwelling		
Linyin Temple		

C. Work in Team.

During the Canton Trade Fair, your company plan to arrange the foreign customers to visit Guangzhou. Try to draw a mind map on ancient architectures in Guangzhou.

183

② Choose a representative from each group to report the mind map to introduce Guangzhou ancient architectures to the foreign customers.